High-Scoring Baseball

Todd Guilliams

Human Kinetics

Library of Congress Cataloging-in-Publication Data

Guilliams, Todd, 1966-
  High-scoring baseball / Todd Guilliams.
    p. cm.
1. Baseball--Scorekeeping. I. Title.
  GV879.G88 2012
  796.357--dc23

                                    2012020608

ISBN-10: 1-4504-1619-5 (print)
ISBN-13: 978-1-4504-1619-1 (print)

Acquisitions Editor: Justin Klug; **Developmental Editor:** Anne Hall; **Assistant Editor:** Tyler Wolpert; **Copyeditor:** Bob Replinger; **Permissions Manager:** Martha Gullo; **Graphic Designer:** Joe Buck; **Graphic Artist:** Tara Welsch; **Cover Designer:** Keith Blomberg; **Photograph (cover):** Robert Williett/Raleigh News & Observer/MCT via Getty Images; **Photographs (interior):** Neil Bernstein, © Human Kinetics, unless otherwise noted; photos on pages 3, 15, 27, 43, 53, 83, 103, 125, 145, 161, 175, 199, and 213 courtesy of B. Kevin Smith, www.PhotoCR.com; **Photo Asset Manager:** Laura Fitch; **Visual Production Assistant:** Joyce Brumfield; **Photo Production Manager:** Jason Allen; **Art Manager:** Kelly Hendren; **Associate Art Manager:** Alan L. Wilborn; **Illustrations:** © Human Kinetics; **Printer:** United Graphics

We thank Valdosta State University in Valdosta, Georgia, for assistance in providing the location for the photo shoot for this book.

Printed in the United States of America   10 9 8 7 6 5 4 3 2 1

The paper in this book is certified under a sustainable forestry program.

Human Kinetics
Website: www.HumanKinetics.com

United States: Human Kinetics
P.O. Box 5076
Champaign, IL 61825-5076
800-747-4457
e-mail: humank@hkusa.com

Canada: Human Kinetics
475 Devonshire Road Unit 100
Windsor, ON N8Y 2L5
800-465-7301 (in Canada only)
e-mail: info@hkcanada.com

Europe: Human Kinetics
107 Bradford Road
Stanningley
Leeds LS28 6AT, United Kingdom
+44 (0) 113 255 5665
e-mail: hk@hkeurope.com

Australia: Human Kinetics
57A Price Avenue
Lower Mitcham, South Australia 5062
08 8372 0999
e-mail: info@hkaustralia.com

New Zealand: Human Kinetics
P.O. Box 80
Torrens Park, South Australia 5062
0800 222 062
e-mail: info@hknewzealand.com

                                                        E5561

This book is dedicated to my family: my mom, Shirley; and dad, Jim; and my brother, Greg; my wife, Julie; and children Casey, Grace, and Wyatt; and my in-laws, Dick and DeDe. What a blessing to have been coached by my father, to have learned how to balance toughness with love from my mother, to have coached alongside my older brother and childhood hero for 22 years, to be married to my high school sweetheart for 20 years, to have had my in-laws' help in reuniting us, and to be the father of three children, who all know Jesus as their Lord and Savior.

1 Thessalonians 5:16-18

Contents

Drill Finder

Drills	SIX ELEMENTS OF OFFENSE						Page
	Bunting	Bat control	Base running	Base stealing	Hitting	Strike zone awareness	
Tee Work					✓		74
Side Flips					✓		76
Underhand Front Toss		✓			✓	✓	78
Batting Practice	✓	✓	✓		✓	✓	80
Statue Bunting	✓						97
One-Knee Bunting	✓						98
Four-Base Bunting	✓						98
Paddle Glove	✓						100
Small Game	✓		✓				100
Baserunning During Batting Practice			✓				120
Intrasquad Games	✓	✓	✓	✓	✓	✓	121
Reads and Reactions at First Base			✓				121
Dive Backs on the Grass				✓			138
Four Man (Stealing Second)				✓			138
Two Man (Stealing Second)				✓			139
Four Man (Stealing Third)				✓			142
Four Man (Stealing Home)				✓			143
Get 'Em Over, Get 'Em In			✓		✓		159

Preface

A productive offense in baseball must have a well-defined game plan. The high-scoring offense has four game-specific goals. If the offense executes just one of those goals and the defense executes one of their four goals, the team will win 90% of its games.

Scoring a lot of runs sounds good, but how can teams, even those with limited natural talent, make it happen? What are the building blocks of a high-powered offense? Every offense wants to have a big inning, but you need to know the components that lead up to it. More important, you need to know how to train both individuals and the team to accomplish that goal. This book is a how-to manual on run production, covering everything from how to score runs to answering the who, what, why, and how of run scoring. It is the culmination of research, observation, and input from outstanding coaches.

A high-scoring offense seeks to score as many runs as possible before the defense can record three outs. Scoring seven or more runs is the primary objective, but a high-scoring offense needs a backup plan that allows the team to score runs when they are not hitting.

The game of baseball, especially the offensive side, is full of failure. Coaches and players need to allow for failure. Productive teams understand not only the right way to execute a skill but also the correct way to fail. *High-Scoring Baseball* presents the three possible outcomes in almost every conceivable situation—the proper execution of the skill, the correct way to fail, and the wrong way to fail.

High-Scoring Baseball details the eight ways to create offensive pressure that give every club the chance to be a high-scoring baseball team. It's a proven system that helps players compete against the game and not their opponent. A player's offensive productivity should be measured not by his batting average but by his ability to obtain one of the eight quality at-bats.

A majority of coaches would agree that the most difficult job is in selling a philosophy to players. One key to selling your offensive philosophy is for it to be rock solid, proven, and backed up by facts. With 18 years of data to support its conclusions, *High-Scoring Baseball* identifies offensive goals for run production, presents ways to identify team strengths, shares facts about run production from college and Major League Baseball, and covers the skills needed to produce runs, such as bunting, baserunning, base stealing, bat control, strike-zone discipline, and hitting. These skills provide an array of weapons that are central to the goal of run scoring.

The book also covers the four offensive plays in baseball—getting on base, moving runners, scoring runs, and sustaining a rally. Practice plans show how to train individual players and teams efficiently. The book concludes with ways to evaluate players using grade cards to help teams stay on track and make adjustments throughout the course of a long season so that the offense can continue to operate at a high level of efficiency.

Acknowledgments

I would like to thank my wife, Julie, for helping me put this book together. Without her journalism expertise, computer skills, and endless patience this book would not have been possible. A special thank you to my brother, Greg, who not only contributed to the content of this book, but also allowed me to spend time on this project through two seasons at Valdosta State.

Thanks to my friends, colleagues, and former players who graciously served as models and did a great job in the South Georgia heat demonstrating skills for both the book and e-book: Greg Guilliams, Mike Croley, Eddie Anderson, Matt Williams, Jake Hicks, and Christian Glisson.

To every coach, professional scout, player, and author from whom I have gained insight on the game of baseball I owe a debt of gratitude.

To my mother, Shirley, and my father, Jim, who taught me never to be afraid to ask questions and gave me the opportunity to play and coach baseball.

Above all, may my Savior and Lord, Jesus Christ, be glorified by my life and lips!

PART I

Offensive Baseball

One of the singular beauties of baseball is that the components of success can be quantified. This can be done in baseball because we have a very measurable result, namely victory, which is created by means of a second, entirely measurable occurrence, that being runs.

   Bill Felber, The Book on the Book

Victories in baseball are the result of outscoring your opponent. Many factors beyond a team's physical talent contribute to its ability to score runs. As coaches and players become better acquainted with the markers of a high-scoring offense identified in this book, they will be better prepared to train those skills and implement the strategies in games.

CHAPTER 1

Facts About Run Production

A team's most precious asset is its allotment of 27 outs. Every at-bat that does not result in an out is a small victory.

Earl Weaver, Hall of Fame manager

Before a discussion about how to score runs can even begin, we need to identify the ways in which runs are produced. After that groundwork is established, the conversation can proceed to assessing personnel, establishing goals, and training players toward those goals. Therefore, our first objective is to take a closer look at how runs are scored. Fortunately, baseball has a wealth of statistical data that we can refer to as we determine how to score runs.

THE MOST IMPORTANT NUMBER IN BASEBALL

One of the unique and endearing aspects of baseball is that, unlike many other popular sports, it does not operate on a clock. When the first pitch of the game is thrown, no one—not players, coaches, umpires, or fans—knows when the contest will end. The single determining factor that affects each half inning of play is the ability of the defense to record three outs. An inning may be as short as three pitches, or it may take an hour, if that is how long it takes the defense to record those three outs.

The most important number in baseball is three. The team on offense can score an unlimited number of runs, right up until the defense records those three outs. Those outs are precious, so our primary objective on offense is to do whatever we can to avoid giving up outs, thereby prolonging the inning and giving ourselves more opportunities to score runs.

Because those three outs are valuable, our offensive system replaces terms like *sacrifice bunts* with the term *kill bunts*. Avoid the mind-set that your team is willing to concede one of its 27 precious outs to gain 90 feet (27.4 m) of ground. For example, our focus is on placing the bunt in a spot that creates pressure on the defense so that they will have trouble recording the out.

DEFINITION OF OFFENSE

The definition of offense is to score as many runs as possible before the other team records three outs. Earl Weaver said that any time a batter reaches base he has won a small victory. Players have many different ways to reach base, to advance runners without giving up outs, and, sometimes, to advance runners with productive outs.

Coaches and players need to understand that there is more to offense than hitting. In some games your team will just not hit well. Whether facing the opponent's staff ace, hitting against the wind blowing in, dealing with a wet field, or playing in a big ballpark, the goal of scoring runs may be daunting because hitting the ball will be more challenging than normal. For this reason every team needs to have a backup plan, which is simply having the ability to score runs when you are not hitting.

An effective backup plan means that a team does anything possible to advance runners around the bases without the benefit of a hit. Some of the hallmarks of an offensive mind-set that includes having a backup plan are earning a base on balls by exercising good strike-zone discipline, stealing a base, taking an extra base on a ball that is put in play, and reading balls in the dirt. Bat-control skills like performing the slash, executing a hit-and-run, and cashing in on limited RBI opportunities by putting the ball in play rather than striking out are also important features of an effective backup plan.

When teams reflect on a game and question why they lost, it is easy to say, "We didn't hit." That often tells only part of the offensive story. Often overlooked in the postgame analysis are the missed opportunities in the form of unproductive outs, bad baserunning, and poor strike-zone discipline. Teams need to train for those days when they are not going to hit. Although nothing is guaranteed, teams that are trained and equipped with an array of offensive skills beyond hitting have a greater chance of scoring a lot of runs. To have an effective offense, a team needs to have a flexible game plan that puts the team in the best possible position, day after day, game after game, to score as many runs as possible. Flexibility means having a game plan and also having a backup plan. As the saying goes, "Plans are everything, and the plan means nothing."

ESTABLISH A RUN GOAL

From 1999 through 2002, the average major-league team scored just under five runs per game. That average varies depending on the level of play, from youth ball to high school and college. Having a point of reference is important, however, and that number—five—plays a key role in establishing goals for runs in a game.

Although five runs is the major-league average, a high-scoring offense will seek to score more than the average number of runs, to be better than average. Each program, at all the various levels of competition, must determine what that aggressive run goal should be. For our college programs at Embry-Riddle, the goal was seven runs, and the results spoke volumes. Over a 13-year period from 1994 through 2006 (see table 1.1), achieving that goal of seven runs per game resulted in a winning percentage of 94%. On the flip side, failure to score seven runs in a game resulted in a winning percentage of just over 50%.

Table 1.1 Seven Run Winning Percentage

Scored seven or more runs	Scored fewer than seven runs
367-25 (94%)	195-158 (55%)

Data from Embry-Riddle Aeronautical University, Daytona Beach, Florida (NAIA).

IMPORTANCE OF THE LEADOFF MAN

One of the many fascinating things about baseball is that with every inning a new offensive player has an opportunity to serve as the leadoff man to start the inning. Each inning is a small game within the game, because at the start of each inning the leadoff man comes to the plate with no runners on and no outs.

"We can think of an inning as the fundamental building block of the game" (Tango, Lichtman, and Dolphin). Emphasizing their desire to win that small skirmish, Florida State University posted a sign in their dugout: "Win Each Inning" during the 2010 College World Series. If winning each inning is the objective, then how important is the leadoff man in that process?

In MLB from 1999 through 2002, if a leadoff man reached base the team had a 95% chance of scoring that inning. If the leadoff man failed to reach base safely, the team's run expectancy (table 1.2) drops to just 30%. That difference is significant, especially in view of the fact that this process repeats itself several times throughout a game. In the 2008 College World Series, when the leadoff man reached base, the team scored 60% of the time.

Table 1.2 Run Expectancy in Major League Baseball

Runners on base	NUMBER OF OUTS	
	0	1
None	.555	.297
Runner on first	.953	.573

BIG-INNING BATTLE

For some offensive teams the goal is to score one run per inning. They hope to achieve this by, as the saying goes, "Get 'em on, get 'em over, get 'em in." A one-run inning is productive, because the offense scored. But this approach often leads to scoring less than the desired number of seven runs. As table 1.3 bears out, the team that achieves the big inning wins far more often than the team that scores just one run per inning.

Our definition of a big inning is scoring three or more runs in a single inning. Playing for a big inning, especially early, in the first two-thirds of the game, makes a lot of sense because we know that in MLB the winning team often scores more runs in a single inning than the losing team does in the entire game. We want to give ourselves every opportunity to get a big inning and not give up outs. Runs are scored in bunches, in a single inning, maybe just once in a nine-inning game. The goal is to have one big inning per game. Having one big inning per game produces a 93% winning percentage, whereas failure to achieve a big inning drops that percentage to just over 50%.

Table 1.3 Game Goal Seven Runs

	Earned	Failed
2006	40-3	9-12
2005	40-2	13-8
2004	40-2	13-8
2003	39-5	9-11
2002	37-2	15-10
Total	196-14	49-49
	93%	55%

Data from Embry-Riddle Aeronautical University, Daytona Beach, Florida (NAIA).

The importance of the big inning was clearly demonstrated by Fresno State, the eventual champions of the 2008 College World Series. The Bulldogs had the most big innings per game (see table 1.4), followed by Georgia, which ranked second and finished as the runner-up.

Table 1.4 2008 College World Series Big Innings

	Team	Games	Big innings	Per game
1	Fresno State	7	8	1.140
2	Georgia	6	6	1.000
4	Stanford	4	4	1.000
8	Florida State	2	2	1.000
6	LSU	3	2	.667
3	North Carolina	5	3	.600
7	Rice	2	1	.500
5	Miami	3	1	.333

Big-Inning Predictors

The definition of a big inning is three or more runs in a single inning. What are some of the predictors of a big inning (table 1.5)? When a big inning occurs in MLB, 75% of the time it includes a walk, a hit-by-pitch, an error, or a stolen base; one of those four events happens in that particular inning for a major-league team to get three runs. We use the term *freebies* to refer to the primary events that lead to a free base: a walk, a hit-by-pitch, an error, or a stolen base. The big inning comes about by more than just a bunch of base hits or a home run. When you understand the predictors, when you understand the components, you start to understand how important it is to draw walks, get hit by a pitch, maybe steal a base, or hit hard line drives that reduce the defenders' reaction time and ultimately might cause errors. Train these four primary freebies in practice and continue to sell to your players the importance of those free 90s.

Table 1.5 2008 NCAA Division I Men's Baseball College World Series Big-Inning Probabilities

Team	Big inning	Freebie	HR	Lead off	Five QABs in a row	Two-strike base hit
Florida State	1		✓			✓
Stanford	2	✓	✓	✓	✓	✓
Georgia	3	✓		✓		
Rice	4	✓	✓	✓	✓	
Fresno State	5	✓	✓	✓	✓	✓
Fresno State	6	✓	✓	✓		✓
LSU	7	✓		✓		✓
North Carolina	8	✓		✓	✓	✓
Miami	9	✓	✓	✓		✓
Florida State	10	✓		✓		✓
Stanford	11		✓	✓		✓
LSU	12	✓				
North Carolina	13			✓	✓	✓
Stanford	14	✓	✓	✓	✓	✓
North Carolina	15	✓	✓	✓		✓
Georgia	16	✓				✓
Georgia	17		✓			✓
Stanford	18	✓	✓	✓		✓
Georgia	19	✓	✓	✓		✓
Fresno State	20	✓	✓	✓	✓	✓
Fresno State	21	✓	✓	✓		✓
Fresno State	22	✓		✓		✓
Fresno State	23	✓	✓	✓	✓	✓
Fresno State	24	✓		✓		✓
Georgia	25	✓		✓		✓
Georgia	26	✓		✓		✓
Fresno State	27	✓	✓			✓
Total		23	16	21	8	24
Percentage		85%	59%	78%	30%	89%

Importance of Two-Strike Hitting

We are going to use an example from the 2008 College World Series as it pertains to the how big innings occur. In the 2008 CWS there were 27 big innings in 17 games played. In those 27 big innings by the various teams, the number one predictor of a big inning was a two-strike base hit (refer to table 1.5). So how important is two-strike hitting?

In MLB 49% of the time batters have two strikes on them when they hit. In the 2008 CWS 48% of the time hitters had two strikes on them. We see a pattern that just about 50% of the time a hitter has two strikes on him. That being the case, two-strike hitting is an important skill to develop because it happens so often. A team's ability to score runs will be greatly affected by its ability to have quality at-bats with two strikes. One of the primary reasons that the University of Georgia was shut out in the 2008 CWS national championship game was their 1-for-17 (6%) performance in quality at-bats (QABs) with two strikes. In comparison, the entire eight-team College World Series field averaged 37% QABs with two strikes (table 1.6).

"(The count) is central to the question of situational batting success because the count is the leverage the batter and pitcher wield against one another in the fight for dominance of the plate" (Felber, 2005). Dominance at the plate for the offensive player is defined by his ability to collect one of the eight types of quality at-bats. Because hitters spend equal time hitting with less than two strikes and with two strikes, they should spend equal time training each skill.

Hitting statistics by count are detailed in table 1.7. The count on the batter often dictates what the pitcher will throw in terms of his repertoire (fastball, curveball, slider, changeup, and so on). The more the count favors the pitcher, the more freedom he has to pitch to all four quadrants of the strike zone and to throw pitches that are less likely to be strikes—the off-speed pitches that often produce weakly hit balls. On the contrary, if the count favors the batter, the hitter is more likely to get a good pitch to hit, usually in the form of a pitch usually thrown for a strike, such as the fastball, because of the pitcher's fear of giving up a base on balls. The walk is second only to the home run in terms of its effectiveness in producing high-scoring baseball. The walk, like the home run, is indefensible. As a result, pitchers try to avoid walks like the plague. As the saying goes, "The tougher the pitch is to hit, the tougher the pitch is to throw."

Table 1.6 Hitting Statistics With Less Than Two Strikes and With Two Strikes, 2008 College World Series

With less than two strikes			With two strikes		
BA	223 / 560	.398	BA	116 / 558	.208
OBP	320 / 657	.487	OBP	186 / 628	.296
QAB%	432 / 684	63%	QAB%	233 / 627	37%

Table 1.7   Hitting Statistics by Count, 2008 College World Series

Count	Batting average	On-base percentage	QAB%
0-0	.418	.430	58%
0-1	.419	.432	62%
1-0	.400	.417	59%
1-1	.391	.404	50%
2-0	.281	.303	64%
2-1	.359	.367	57%
3-0	.000	.974	97%
3-1	.520	.833	88%
0-2	.189	.198	25%
1-2	.166	.183	26%
2-2	.224	.242	32%
3-2	.271	.536	62%

You can explain the correct offensive approach in simple terms. For example, with less than two strikes, "When ahead, never late" is a useful catchphrase because the hitter will get more fastballs to hit. Conversely, with two strikes, "When behind, never early" is the catchphrase to remember because when the pitcher is ahead in the count, a batter will see more off-speed pitches to hit.

In the four counts involving two strikes, comprising 48% of all sample events, the collective batting average was .208 with an accompanying on-base percentage of .296 and the quality at-bat percentage was 37%. In the eight other counts, which comprise 52% of the sample, the collective batting average was .398 with a .487 OBP and a QAB% of 63%.

Staring at this study, I am drawn to one conclusion . . . the role of aggressiveness in offensive success. That would not have been my anticipation going into it. Like a lot of people, I would have counseled patience at the plate. But as the discussion relates to batting average (and ultimately quality at-bats) . . . the evidence argues to the contrary. Based on the data, the most hittable pitches are very likely to be among the first two a batter sees (Felber, 2005).

Avoiding the Double Play

A pitcher's best friend is a double play—one pitch, two outs. The other side of the coin is that the offense needs to do everything it can to avoid hitting into a double play. A sound offensive plan includes strategies such as a well-placed bunt, a steal, a slash, a hit-and-run, using the shade, and starting the runner when the batter has a 3-2 count. Another weapon that the offense needs to employ to avoid the double play is to make sure that base runners advance on balls in the dirt. This skill has really come of age in the last decade. Base runners are being taught to be more aggressive on balls in the dirt, forcing the catcher to block the ball, pick it up, and throw out the runner.

With a man on first base and no outs, the batter is in a great situation to take a shot to right. This play is effective for three reasons. For starters, the first baseman is holding the runner, which leaves a big area, a "canyon," between him and the second baseman. The second baseman also has to cheat toward second to cover the double play or a possible steal, widening the hole even more. Second, by hitting the ball to the second baseman's left, the batter is less likely to hit into a double play. Third, if the ball is hit through the right side into the outfield, the runner usually continues to third base.

The strategy for a left-handed hitter would be to hook the ball into the four hole, or hit the outside part of the ball. A right-handed hitter would attack the inside part of the ball and carve the baseball into the four hole. The left-handed hitter may want to crowd the plate to be able to handle the outside strike more effectively, whereas the right-handed batter may want to back off the plate to be better able to handle the inside fastball.

Other factors that determine whether the offense has a propensity to hit into double plays are the characteristics of the athletes. The faster the running speed of the team is, the less likely they are to hit into double plays. A team with more hitters who hit fly balls rather than ground balls will reduce the opposing team's opportunities to turn double plays. Finally, opposing pitchers

Practice Tip

Teach hitters the "1-2-3" contact points of a baseball. Right-handed hitters attack a "1" with a runner at first base, whereas left-handed hitters attack a "3" with a runner at first base. Hitting is about managing failure. By focusing on a "1," or the inside part of the ball, if the hitter fails he usually hits a "2" and still hits the ball squarely. But if he tries to hit a "2," misses, and hits a "3," the result is generally a weak ground ball. This imagery (figure 1.1) helps reinforce the concept of attacking the inside part of the ball. We often say, "Attack a 1."

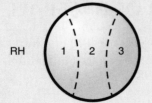
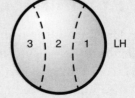

Figure 1.1 1-2-3 contact points.

who can locate pitches down in the zone with movement will cause batters to hit more ground balls that can be turned into double plays.

When runners are on base, the hitter needs to have a heightened awareness of attacking the inside part of the baseball. This approach helps the hitter stay through the baseball and lends itself to hitting more line drives and the occasional fly ball. The opposite approach would be to strike the outside part of the baseball and hit ground balls, which might turn into double plays. The pitcher will try to entice the batter to hit ground balls. Some pitchers have the ability to sink the baseball, which produces more ground balls because hitters have a tendency to hit the top of the baseball. As a result, hitters who face sinkerball pitchers have two options: (a) get beneath the sinker or (b) wait until the pitcher elevates the sinker.

There are three cardinal sins in hitting:

1. Taking a first-pitch fastball for a strike
2. Hitting into a double play in a positive count
3. Taking a called third strike

Note that of the three cardinal sins in hitting, one is hitting into a double play. The hitter must learn to drive the ball into the gaps when the count is in his favor and not roll over the baseball when he is behind in the count, which can result in a double play.

Odds of Three Consecutive Hits

The odds of getting three consecutive hits in any one inning are 27:1. Considering those odds, the offense should employ additional tactics besides just trying to get base hits to achieve the goal of having a big inning—scoring three or more runs in a single inning. Recognizing how difficult it is to get three consecutive hits, we see the importance of walks, HBPs, stolen bases, and errors. Productive offensive players get on base and drive in runs. They understand that the goal of every plate appearance is not always to try to get a base hit but rather to achieve a quality at-bat for the team.

PYTHAGOREAN THEOREM OF BASEBALL

Developed by Bill James, the Pythagorean theorem of baseball states that a ballclub's winning percentage should be equal to the square of the number of runs scored divided by the sum of the square of the number of runs scored and the number of runs allowed:

$$\text{Winning percentage} = \frac{(\text{runs scored})^2}{[(\text{runs scored})^2 + (\text{runs allowed})^2]}$$

The theory (demonstrated in table 1.8) is that in baseball, the greater the run differential is while maintaining low scores, the more likely a team is to win (www.everything2.com, 2008).

The goal of high-scoring baseball is to maximize run production by using the points detailed in this book, such as getting the leadoff man on base, hitting effectively with two strikes, achieving a big inning, and accumulating free bases. By entering the team's run data for the previous year into James' formula, coaches can evaluate their team's performance to help set specific run production goals for the upcoming season.

Table 1.8 Actual Data vs. Pythagorean Theorem

Year	Runs scored	Runs against	Games	Record	Win%	PT%	PT record	+/-
2006	466	219	64	49-15	.766	.819	52-13	−3
2005	503	189	63	53-10	.841	.876	55-8	−2
2004	499	225	63	53-10	.841	.831	52-12	+1
2003	479	239	64	48-16	.750	.796	51-13	−3
2002	510	232	64	52-12	.828	.829	53-11	−1

Data from Embry-Riddle Aeronautical University, Daytona Beach, Florida (NAIA).

PT% = Pythagorean theorem winning percentage; PT record = Pythagorean theorem record; +/− = difference between Win% and PT%.

FREE BASES

The four key types of free bases are the walk, the hit-by-pitch, the stolen base, and an error by the defense, although there are others, such as a base runner advancing on a wild pitch or going from first to third on a single, that is, gaining an extra base. For our discussion, we will focus on these four key free bases. Brian Shoop, the astute head coach at University of Alabama at Birmingham who won the national NAIA championship with Birmingham Southern in 2002, is the first person whom I heard refer to the accumulation of free bases as being critical to the ability to score runs.

The idea goes back to the makeup of a big inning. Seventy-five percent of big innings at the major-league level include a walk, a hit-by-pitch, an error, or a stolen base. Against better teams you have to earn those, even though the name *free bases* implies that they are something that a team is given, that they did not earn. The freebie (table 1.9) is sometimes compared to a turnover in football, and turnovers are certainly critical in that sport because they can change the tide of the game.

In baseball one of the predictors of which team will score the most runs is which team accumulates the most free bases. Generally, the greater the differential in freebies is, the greater the run differential is. We are talking

Table 1.9   Freebie War

	2007		2008		2009	
	27-30		36-18-1		43-21	
	VSU	Opp	VSU	Opp	VSU	Opp
BB	185	244	196	168	276	200
HBP	69	51	87	63	138	62
SB	61	84	70	43	61	59
E	100	101	62	91	99	108
	−65 −1.14/g		+108 +1.96/g		+163 +2.55/g	

about 90 feet (27.4 m)—a free 90, so to speak—and you have to get around the bases before you score, so whoever can amass the most free 90s will have the greater opportunity to score more runs. You need to knock in those runs or the defense has to let them in; you want to maximize those runs on offense and minimize them on defense. When we talk about realistic goals, we will set some goals for free bases per game. At the end of the game, whoever won the freebie war likely scored the most runs.

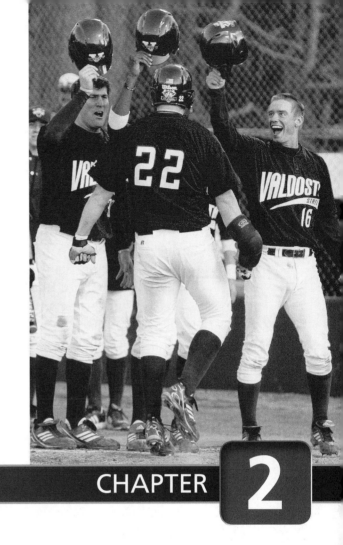

CHAPTER 2

Assessing Your Personnel

Knowing your players is one of your most important jobs. What we're hoping for in evaluating our players is to play the right athletes in the right positions and the right situations.

Andy Lopez, head baseball coach, University of Arizona

TOOLS EVALUATION

Accurately assessing players' athletic ability, skill level, and baseball instincts is critical in determining the style of offense that a team will employ to maximize offensive productivity. The goal of a high-scoring offense is to score seven runs per game regardless of those factors, but the approach will vary. A starting point is to evaluate a player's tools. The five tools of a baseball player are running speed; hitting for power, which is measured in home runs and a high slugging percentage; hitting, which is measured in batting average; fielding; and throwing. Some professional organizations have added a sixth tool to the traditional five: strike-zone discipline. Focusing on offensive production, we are going to concentrate on hitting, hitting for power, speed, and strike-zone awareness.

The following tests help us measure the proficiency of our players in those areas:

1. Speed
   a. 60-yard (55 m) dash: The average MLB runner runs the distance in 7.0 seconds
   b. Steal of second: Time players from a steal lead through second base standing up. A good steal time from a typical 12-foot (3.7 m) lead from first base and sliding into second base would be 3.4 seconds or less.
   c. Through first base: The average MLB left-handed batter reaches first base in 4.2 seconds; the average MLB right-handed batter needs 4.3 seconds.
2. Power can be assessed by measuring the exit velocity of a ball coming off a batter's bat. An easy way to measure it is to perform side toss and have the batter use a wood bat. A person with a radar gun stands behind the batter and captures the ball exiting the bat. A good exit speed for a college player with a wood bat is 90 miles per hour (145 km/h). The test does not guarantee that the person with 90-plus exit speed will hit home runs, but it does say that the batter who can hit the ball with proper trajectory and correct timing has the potential to hit home runs. Bat speed in the range of 86 to 89 miles per hour (138 to 143 km/h), along with proper hitting mechanics and timing, is sufficient to catch up with most college pitching.

Exit Speed Guidelines for College Players

92-99 miles per hour (148-159 km/h) = HR power

88-91 (142-146) = gap-to-gap power

83-87 (134-140) = singles hitter with occasional doubles pop

80-82 (129-132) = struggles to hit pitches with velocity above 85 miles per hour

3. Bat control can be tested by assessing a batter's proficiency at hitting hard ground balls that stay fair to the back side of the field and strike the grass first. The first bounce must not hit the dirt circle in front of home plate. If the hitter can perform this skill consistently, he has demonstrated an ability to control the barrel with correct timing. To perform this skill correctly, a hitter must do four things that are critical in the function of a good swing:

a. Keep the barrel above the flight of the pitch.

b. The barrel must strike the inside part of the ball.

c. Stay through the baseball or have great extension.

d. Let the ball travel the proper distance.

The first round of batting practice is a good way to implement this test because it forces hitters to let the ball travel deep into the strike zone and use proper swing mechanics to execute the skill. Have the players hit three of five line drives down off the grass to the backside of the field before they are allowed to free swing. After a player has executed three repetitions out of five swings, he "graduates" and is free to proceed with batting practice. This skill is important because the same skills are needed to move runners, execute a hit-and-run, and hit with two strikes. This simple but challenging test allows you to find out the bat control proficiency of your hitters.

A suitable frequency for performing this drill is about three days a week, not every day. As players become more proficient at it, they will be able to move more quickly through the batting-practice (BP) routine. What may take five rounds to accomplish at the beginning of the year will be done in one round later in the season.

4. Tracking players' strike-zone awareness can be done by charting them in batting practice and games. Keep track of any ball that a hitter swings at that is outside the strike zone. The average major-league hitter chases pitches outside the strike zone about 21% of the time. Players and coaches can use this baseline standard when evaluating players' ability to swing at strikes and take balls. In the 2008 College World Series, the University of Miami team chased pitches outside the strike zone just 8% of the time. The Hurricanes were disciplined in their ability to get a good pitch to hit. Strike-zone awareness is critical because it has a direct correlation to on-base percentage, which translates into base runners and, ultimately, runs scored.

Practice Tip

Use either a catcher or a square strike-zone net during batting practice so that the coach throwing BP or someone charting the BP can better gauge a hitter's pitch selection. This approach will help simulate a game and allows some evaluation of whether a hitter is swinging at balls outside the zone or taking strikes.

DEER OR BUFFALO

After assessing players' ability level, coaches can start to place players into groups with similar skill levels. For example, creating two groups with names such as "deer" for the speed group and "buffalo" for the slower group can be a way for coaches to divide their players based on their running speed. This method is useful because it can help with planning practice. For example, the coach may decide to spend more time with the deer on straight steals, whereas the buffalo would work on delay steals. Another example would be for the deer to work on stealing third, while the buffalo spend time on recognizing and reacting to balls in the dirt. The buffalo need to key in on lateral movement to advance to third on a dirt ball. This key will help them avoid being thrown out on a ball that kicks just in front of the catcher. Dirt ball reads are critical for the buffalo group because they provide opportunities for base runners to get to third without straight stealing. Another way to target the training for the deer and buffalo is for deer to spend more time bunting while buffalo spend more time hitting. The deer, because they can run, should spend more time on bat-control skills such as the hit-and-run, whereas the buffalo should spend more time on driving in runs and hitting with men in scoring position. Putting a label on players is a way for them to take pride in their skill set, and it reinforces how they can contribute to a high-scoring offense.

Deer	Buffalo
Straight steal	Delay steal
Drag and push bunts	Sacrifice bunt
Hit-and-run	Hit-and-run drive
Get 'em over	Drive 'em over
Safety squeeze (runner at third)	Fly ball with the infield in

BATTING ORDER

The ultimate batting order would consist of power, speed, bat control, proper mental approach, and a blend of left-handed and right-handed batters. Here is a look at some of the criteria for each person in the batting order:

Leadoff Batter　The leadoff batter should possess outstanding strike-zone discipline, speed, and baserunning instincts and be one of your two best overall hitters. You want your leadoff hitter to be an exceptional hitter because he will usually get one extra at-bat per game. The leadoff batter must be able to hit above-average velocity so that he can handle the opposing team's closer. He must also be able to make a statement that he can handle the starting pitcher's best fastball when starting the game. His success will give his teammates a confidence boost and make the pitcher doubt the quality of his fastball. For argument's sake let's say that our leadoff batter bats right-handed.

Two Hole   The two-hole hitter is the most underappreciated batter in the lineup. Most ballclubs make the mistake of putting a hitter in the two hole who is predominately a bat-control hitter but not an outstanding pure hitter. A high-scoring offense needs to have a two-hole hitter who defines the offense, meaning that he can not only handle the bat but also strike fear in the other team because he has at least gap-to-gap power, if not home run power. If your team has a two-hole hitter who is a move-the-runner guy and you're hoping that he can just bunt and draw an occasional walk, keep in mind that your opponent's pitching staff will dominate that hitter, especially late in the ballgame, because he will be challenged in the strike zone and the corners will play up, negating the bunt. He will be forced to swing the bat to earn his way onto base. In our ideal lineup, the two-hole hitter will bat left-handed and be able to take advantage of the hole on the right side created when our leadoff batter gets on base.

Three Hole   The three-hole position is usually reserved for your best line-drive hitter. But the three-hole hitter does not have to be your best RBI producer. The four-hole hitter will have more RBI opportunities than the three-hole hitter. The third batter should possess good strike-zone discipline because he will be pitched tough in RBI situations. He must learn to swing at pitches in his zone and not chase pitches outside the strike zone. It is advantageous for the third hitter to draw walks because that puts him on base for your RBI producers—the hitters in the four, five, and six slots. Again, alternating batters is advantageous for your high-scoring offense, so we want the third batter to hit from the opposite side of the fourth batter.

Cleanup   The four-hole hitter is someone who possesses power, is a great RBI producer, and essentially is a hitter who is feared. The four-hole hitter is the cornerstone of the offense. When placing personnel in a batting order the ideal place to start is with the four-hole hitter. A batter with 90-plus bat speed and a line-drive up stroke with a great approach would fit the profile. If the three-hole hitter bats right-handed, the four-hole hitter would ideally bat left-handed and vice versa.

Five Hole   The five-hole hitter's job is to drive in runs. Although he may not possess the best strike-zone discipline, he can make up for that with aggressiveness and an ability to drive balls to the gaps. The ideal five-hole hitter is different from the four-hole hitter in terms of his ability to handle the bat. For example, if the four-hole hitter has excellent strike-zone discipline, having a five-hole hitter who occasionally chases pitches would be acceptable. But if the four-hole hitter is vulnerable to a right-handed breaking ball, the ideal five-hole hitter would be able to handle that pitch. If both hitters have the same issue, it becomes too easy for the opposing pitcher to strike out both hitters in critical RBI situations.

Six Hole   The sixth batter is similar to the fifth batter in that both can drive in runs, but the six-hole hitter strikes out more often than the four and five hitters. In a perfect world he would possess at least gap-to-gap power and have different strengths and weaknesses than the fifth batter. If the five-hole batter hits right-handed, the ideal six-hole hitter would bat left-handed. Alternating hitters really challenges the opposing pitcher to command all his pitches in all quadrants of the strike zone, and he cannot get into easy patterns of striking out similar batters. For example, a predominantly right-handed lineup facing a right-handed pitcher with a good slider who can locate that pitch on the outer half of the plate will likely struggle because pitches are breaking sharply away from them. Without left-handed hitting, an offense has nothing to counteract that pitch and force the pitcher to do something different.

Seven Hole   The seven-hole batter would be a good spot for a leadoff-type hitter, someone who possesses speed but is not quite as good a hitter as the leadoff batter. He knows how to run the bases and can set the table for the bottom of the lineup. He does not have to possess power, but ideally he can steal a base and help propel himself around the bases. This batter would bat right-handed in the ideal batting lineup.

Eight and Nine   The last two spots in the batting order are reserved for the weakest hitters in terms of their ability to hit for average. These two hitters should be proficient in their ability to get a bunt down and execute bat-control skills such as a hit-and-run. The eight and nine hitters probably play critical defensive positions such as shortstop, second base, center field, or catcher. Ideally, the last two batters should bat from opposite sides. If the hitters are similar, the preference would be for the nine-hole batter to be the better runner because after the lineup flips to the top, the nine-hole hitter might be able to steal a base, go first to third, and score from first base on a ball hit into the gap.

Table 2.1 shows the ultimate batting lineup and the ideal skill sets to field a diverse and well-rounded starting nine. We have seven offensive skills to work with, and we've limited the model to just three or four skills for each of the nine hitters. The more talented your ballclub is, the more skills your players are going to bring to the table—and vice versa.

Table 2.1   Batting Order Criteria

	Bat	Speed	Hit	Power	Bunt	Bat control	RBI	Strike-zone awareness
1	S	✓	✓		✓			✓
2	L	✓		✓		✓		
3	R		✓				✓	✓
4	L		✓	✓			✓	
5	R		✓	✓			✓	
6	L			✓		✓	✓	
7	R				✓	✓		✓
8	L	✓			✓	✓		
9	R	✓			✓			✓

FLEXIBLE AND MULTIFACETED

An offense that is multifaceted is proficient in the art of the eight offensive skills:

1. Base stealing
2. Baserunning
3. Bat-control skills
4. Situational hitting
5. Hitting
6. Hitting for power
7. Short game (bunting)
8. Strike-zone discipline

Each member of the offense must repeatedly practice and improve all these elements of an offense for a team to increase their chances of scoring runs consistently. Although not every player will have the talent or skill to master all these areas, a team that has these elements present can form a productive offensive unit. This versatility is valuable when facing different types of pitchers, such as a

1. soft lefty,
2. velocity righty,
3. backward guy (throws curveballs in fastball counts),

4. pitcher with no off-speed command, and

5. Friday night guy (has it all—velocity and a quality secondary pitch with command).

A well-equipped offensive unit possesses the necessary tools to contend effectively with myriad of situations and pitchers.

A flexible game plan can be adjusted after the game starts. The adage "Planning is everything, and the plan means nothing" applies to game day. The offense will have a plan going into the game about how to dismantle the starting pitcher, but if the pitcher changes his usual patterns or has great command of a curveball when he typically does not, the offense has to be able to adjust. The offense might struggle to hit when a pitcher has good command of a quality secondary pitch such as curveball and will have to emphasize skills such as the short game and aggressive baserunning and base stealing. They will need to demonstrate great strike-zone discipline by taking the curveball below the strike zone. An offense that is flexible will be able to adapt its approach and adjust to what the defense is giving them. The ability to adjust is what separates mediocre offenses from great ones. Having a toolbox full of instruments to attack different game situations is highly advantageous.

STRENGTHS AND WEAKNESSES

Players' strengths and weakness will be revealed if they are tested in practice through challenging game-speed drills. Competitive drills are ones that reveal a weakness that, with drill repetition, can be turned into a strength. Coaches who know their players' strengths and weaknesses are better equipped to know which skills each player will be able to execute in games. For example, a player who has struggled to execute a hit-and-run in practice should not be asked to execute a hit-and-run in a game. When a player is proficient at a skill such as a drag bunt, the coach would be more inclined to ask him to execute that skill in a game.

Weaknesses should be worked on in a practice setting but not applied in a game if at all possible. A player will break down at his weakest link in the heat of battle. To get better, a player needs to spend time working on a weakness until it becomes a strength. The coach who knows his players' strengths and plays to those strengths gives the team the best chance to score runs that day. Competitive drills and intra-squad game are the best way to reveal strengths and weaknesses.

Best Nine

Play your best nine, not your nine best.

Skip Bertman, head baseball coach, Louisiana State University

Some players bring out the best in their teammates, causing them to play at a higher level collectively than they would individually. Synergy means "working together," but synergism is more than that. According to legendary coach Skip Bertman, "It means two or more people working together in a way that their combined power is more than just the sum of their individual power." In his book, *The Magic of Teamwork,* Pat Williams illustrates synergism through a horse-pulling contest at a county fair. The first-place horse pulled a sled weighing 4,500 pounds (2,040 kg), and the second-place horse pulled 4,000 pounds (1,810 kg). The owners calculated that the two horses together could pull 8,500 pounds (3,850 kg), so they put it to a test. To their surprise, the owners found that the two horses hitched together pulled 12,000 pounds (5,440 kg)—3,500 pounds (1,590 kg) more than the sum of their individual efforts. That effort demonstrates synergism.

One of the greatest challenges for any coach is to find out which nine players play the best together. All teams need a catalyst, a player who is the sparkplug of the team. This player may not be the most talented, but he is the one who elevates the group. That quality may take the form of leadership, enthusiasm, determination, or toughness. Baseball is a team game wrapped up in individual performances. The batter–pitcher confrontation is a good example of an individual performance that affects the rest of the team. An offensive unit that demonstrates synergy fueled by a catalyst will outperform their competition on a regular basis. Although executing skills is important, it is secondary to true teamwork.

Personnel Options

A typical high school may struggle to have a 24-man roster of highly skilled offensive players. College teams, for whom recruiting is essential, have a greater chance of having more than one skilled player at each position. Having options in the form of left-handed hitting and right-handed hitting is a useful luxury. For example, being able to bring a pinch hitter off the bench for a light-hitting shortstop or bringing a left-handed hitter to the plate against a right-handed sinkerball pitcher can be the difference in the ballgame. In addition, having depth creates competition for playing time, which pushes players to a higher level of performance.

Competition brings out the best in some players and the worst in others. Having options going into a ballgame is critical when putting the pieces of the puzzle together and trying to score seven runs per game. Creating the right matchup gives your team a better opportunity to come through in a specific game situation. Having various types of players who possess different skill sets, such as power, speed, bat left-handed, bat right-handed, and ability to hit a plus fastball and a curveball, gives your team diversity and an offense that is hard to defend.

Intangibles

Casey Stengel, the famed former manager of the New York Yankees and New York Mets said, "I want players with brains and guts." Beyond the talents of hitting, running speed, and hitting for power, baseball is a game that values players who possess baseball instincts and courage. Baseball also rewards players who can anticipate the next move of their opponent. Coaches who can determine which players possess baseball instincts are fortunate. The player who can anticipate what pitches he might get during an at-bat or when a pitcher is going to the plate so that he can get a great jump on a steal attempt, the player who recognizes when a ball is going to drop in front of an outfielder so that he can take an extra base, or the player who recognizes when the defense is playing back so that he can drop down a bunt to reach base is a valuable offensive player. Baseball does require great physical tools, but it rewards the player who has finely tuned fundamentals. Baseball is played by people who vary in height from 5 feet, 5 inches (165 cm) to 6 feet, 10 inches (208 cm) because each position requires a variety of skill sets and talents. A superior offensive player has talent, skill, great baseball instincts, and outstanding makeup. A player who possesses brains and guts is a valuable offensive commodity.

Home Ballpark

Tailoring your offense to be productive at home is advantageous because in baseball at least half your games will be played in your home ballpark. For example, if your ballpark is spacious, then speed would benefit your team. The reverse would also be true: A smaller ballpark would favor the team that has big, strong guys who can hit for power. Teams want to be balanced, but a team needs to be equipped to score runs at home. Finding ways to score runs in your home ballpark is where your team needs to start.

Many natural conditions, such as wind, play a factor in how far the ball travels. If the home ballpark is at sea level and the wind typically blows in, home runs will likely be rare. As a result, the offense would emphasize a line-drive stroke and use the short game and base stealing as offensive weapons. The opposite would be true if the home ballpark is located well above sea level, like the Colorado Rockies' home park; the home team would like to have power because the frequency of home runs would be far greater.

CHAPTER **3**

Setting Realistic Goals

We made sure that all 10 to 12 offensive goals fit our philosophy. We did the same for defense and the kicking game. We set a series of specific goals for each area, a practice many people don't think about and might not consider as important as we did.

Tom Osborne, former head football coach, University of Nebraska

Tom Osborne led the University of Nebraska to three NCAA Division I football national championships and 25 bowl games. In the quest to become a high-scoring offense, establishing and then measuring offensive goals are critical components to winning games. These goals are critical for players and coaches to track and measure on a game-by-game basis to provide the impetus for adjustments. Establishing goals is important not only because they provide direction for the offense but also because they help players adjust their focus from playing against an opponent to playing against the game. Based on the evidence that we have collected, the knowledge that an offense has the chance to win 90% of its games when the team executes just one of their four offensive goals should help the players be confident in themselves and the system, allowing them to focus on the things that they can control.

ESTABLISHING FUNDAMENTAL OFFENSIVE GOALS

Measuring goals that affect run scoring will reveal whether you win or lose the game. After countless hours of research we have established four offensive goals. These building blocks of a high-scoring baseball team are (1) score seven runs, (2) produce one big inning, (3) accumulate nine freebies, and (4) tally 50% quality at-bats (figure 3.1). Research with our teams over the past two decades has shown that achieving one of these goals on offense and achieving one of our four goals on defense has resulted in victory in 90% of our games. But when we get shut out, achieving zero goals on either the offensive or the defensive side of the ledger, our winning percentage slips under 50%.

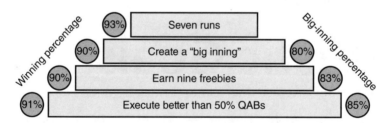

Figure 3.1 Four building blocks of a high-scoring offense.

Zero Sum

The game of baseball has been called a zero-sum game. Scoring runs is not enough; you also have to prevent runs from scoring. The bottom line is that teams can't win 90% of their games on offense alone. With that in mind, we also have four defensive goals that are opposites of the offensive goals. We mention this briefly to explain that defense is an important component to a successful team, although we will not cover it in detail in this book. Those defensive goals are (1) allow four or fewer runs, (2) surrender four or fewer freebies, (3) throw 150 or fewer pitches, and (4) prevent the big inning in a nine-inning game.

Displaying your game goals in your locker room is a useful approach. Players need to understand that these goals are the building blocks of a high-scoring baseball team. They provide direction before the game and serve as the criteria on which the offense will be evaluated after each game as the season moves along.

Seven Runs

In a nine-inning ballgame, our goal is to score seven runs. As previously stated, achieving the goal of seven runs has historically resulted in our ballclub winning 93% of our games (table 3.1). Seven runs is the goal that worked for our team, in our situation, but when striving to set a realistic goal for runs, each program needs to assess many factors, such as personnel, competition, field conditions, weather, and players' age and skill level. The bottom line is that each team must have a benchmark that they are striving for every game.

Some may argue that seven runs is an unrealistic goal, especially in certain situations such as when your team is facing an opponent's staff ace. Friday night in the SEC provides evidence to the contrary, however, showing that even at the highest levels of the college game seven runs is a realistic goal. In 2006, en route to winning its first Southeastern Conference regular-season title in over 100 years, the University of Kentucky baseball team averaged well over seven runs per game on Friday nights versus SEC pitching. Typically, on a Friday night when two SEC teams face each other, both teams feature their staff ace in hopes of winning the first game of a three-game series. Most baseball observers would likely presume that a game featuring the teams' top pitchers would be a low-scoring affair, but the Kentucky Wildcats proved that theory wrong by scoring an average of nine runs in their Friday night matchups. The SEC average that year on Friday nights was 5.8.

Table 3.1   Seven Runs (1994-2009)

Seven runs	Less than seven runs
456-31	195-158

One Big Inning

The next building block in our high-scoring goal pyramid, after scoring seven runs, is the goal of producing one big inning in a nine-inning ballgame. The single most significant contributor to the ability of an offense to score seven runs is producing one big inning in a game. Scoring one run every inning for the entire contest is extremely difficult, and we have already seen in Major League Baseball that most of the time, the winning team scores more runs in a single inning than the losing team does in the entire game. Playing for the big inning in the first two-thirds of the game makes sense for this reason. For every big inning surrendered while on defense, a team must produce two big innings to regain the advantage. In simpler terms, a team that accumulates a big inning will typically win the game as long as the defense does not yield a big inning to their opponent (table 3.2).

Table 3.2   Big-Inning Battle

	Achieved (big inning)	Not achieved (big inning)
2006	40-3	9-12
2005	40-2	13-8
2004	40-2	13-8
2003	39-5	9-11
2002	37-2	15-10
Total	196-14	49-49
	93%	55%

Data from Embry-Riddle Aeronautical University, Daytona Beach, Florida (NAIA).

Nine Freebies

Seventy-five percent of the time, a big inning contains a free base in the form of a walk, hit-by-pitch, error, or stolen base. Hence, the third building block in the goal pyramid is the accumulation of freebies because they in turn feed the big inning. An offense needs to find a way to accumulate a minimum of nine free bases in a nine-inning ballgame. Simple math says that teams need to average one free base per inning or that each offensive player needs to be responsible for achieving one free base. Free bases are critical to high-scoring baseball: Freebies feed the big inning, and the big inning has a profound effect on the chances of winning. Remember, the odds of getting three consecutive hits in any one single inning are 27:1. Because the odds do not favor the offense in terms of consecutive hits in a single inning, accumulating at least one free base in the inning will help produce the big inning and ultimately assist the offense in arriving at seven runs.

While the offense is trying to accumulate nine freebies, when on defense the same team must work to yield no more than four freebies to their opponent. These goals are challenging on both sides of the ball, and the offensive and defensive components cannot work independently of one another. Teams should strive to have their offense on the positive side of the freebie war by a margin of five. Some may ask, "Why make an allowance for the defense to yield four free bases?" It comes back to establishing realistic goals. For example, in MLB the average pitching staff allows just over three base on balls per game and the defense makes less than one error per game. Holding opponents to four free bases per game in all four categories is challenging. Freebies are similar to turnovers in football: Whoever collects the most generally wins the game.

Fifty Percent Quality At-Bats

For the past 16 years we have kept track of our team's ability to accumulate quality at-bats. We have found that accumulating 50% quality at-bats (QABs) is a realistic goal and a critical step necessary for the offense to score seven runs per game. A typical game in which the offense is in position to score seven runs would consist of approximately 40 plate appearances. For the offensive team to hit the benchmark of 50% QABs, they would need to have 20 quality at-bats. For example, each individual player, if he has four at-bats during the game, would have to achieve quality at-bats in two of his four plate appearances. Although all QABs help produce runs, not all of them produce immediate runs, like a home run does. Therefore, an offense could have four QABs in an inning and not record a run. Every spectator has seen a potential rally end when a batter uses a poor approach and hits into an inning-ending double play. Although accumulating quality at-bats is important, equally important is stringing them together, particularly five in a row, because a sequence of that length can lead to a big inning.

SUCCESS IS IN THE MIX

Although the focus of this book is to explore the art of prolific run production, the ultimate goal is to achieve victory. With that outcome in mind, achieving the goals that we have set forth for the offense and defense will produce a magnificent winning percentage (table 3.3). Figure 3.2 provides clear evidence of the effect of meeting those goals in achieving high-scoring baseball and, ultimately, winning baseball games. The team that achieves zero goals on offense and zero on defense will have a losing record, yet achieving just one goal on each side of the ledger will produce at least a 90% winning percentage. Achieving two goals of the four on each side of the ledger has proved to be 99% effective.

Table 3.3 Overall Record When Achieving One of the Four Offensive Game Goals

Offense	Achieved (2005)	Not achieved (2005)	Achieved (2006)	Not achieved (2006)
Seven runs	34-2	15-3	35-1	18-9
Big inning +3	40-3	9-12	40-2	13-8
Freebies +9	23-3	26-12	30-4	23-6
50% QAB	25-0	24-15	22-0	21-10

Data from Embry-Riddle Aeronautical University, Daytona Beach, Florida (NAIA).

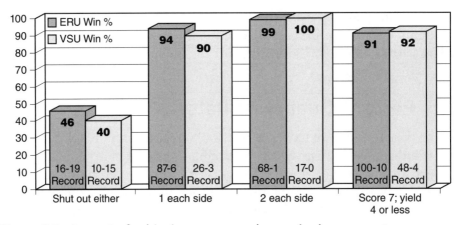

Figure 3.2 Impact of achieving game goals on winning percentage.

Achieving the goal of either scoring seven runs on offense or allowing four runs on defense produces a winning percentage above 90%. Although scoring runs is our focus here, offense is only half the game when it comes to who ultimately emerges as the victor. Success is certainly in the mix; achieving one goal on each side of the ledger is a realistic and proven formula for success in terms of victories. We want to set realistic goals, but we also want them to be challenging. Players need to believe in their ability to achieve those goals and not worry about the other team. We do not have control over the other team's pitcher, the umpire, the weather, or the fans, so instead we want to focus our attention on achieving our offensive goals regardless of the competition.

OFFENSIVE PRESSURE

Creating offensive pressure is essential in the offensive scheme of a high-scoring baseball team because pressure can create miscues on the defense. The components that make up the building blocks of a high-scoring offense include the following skills:

Goal	Per game
Stolen bases	3
QAB% with runners in scoring position	50%
Two-strike QAB%	37%
Chase percentage	<21%
Leadoff man reaches	67% (6 of 9 innings)
Opponent's pitch count	>150
3-to-8 (hard hit balls)	50%
BBs and HBPs	6

Stolen Bases

The offense that gains 90 feet (27.4 m) without giving up an out has executed a productive play. The stolen base is the classic way to accomplish gaining a free 90 feet. In a 1987 interview Hall of Famer Tom Seaver wisely observed, "Lou Brock and Maury Wills are probably the two players most responsible for the biggest change in the game over the last 15 years—the stolen base." They helped revolutionize the game by perfecting the art of the stolen base and convincing baseball purists of the value of the stolen base in regard to run scoring. Teams that like to run create pressure not only with the stolen base but also through the threat of the stolen base because it distracts the pitcher. The pitcher has to focus on the runner, which divides his thinking and focus between the base runner and hitter. As a result, even if the base runner does not attempt a steal, the batter will get better pitches to hit in the form of elevated pitches because pitchers try to be quick to the plate and tend to leave the ball up in the zone. "Maury Wills started a trend with his 104 steals in 1962. . . . Maury is a phenomenon of modern baseball. He is an all-time master at getting on and around the bases on his own momentum," noted Jackie Robinson in a 1966 edition of *Sport Magazine*. A lofty but realistic goal for stolen bases per game would be three. A high-scoring offense wants to go into the game thinking that it can achieve the goal of three stolen bases regardless of the competition.

Stealing bases is contingent on three factors:

1. The runner's speed and jump—3.4 seconds or less is a good time from the lead at first base to sliding into second base.
2. The pitcher's delivery time to the plate—1.4 seconds or longer is considered slow, which is a green light for base runners.
3. The catcher's throwing time to second base—2.1 seconds or longer is considered below average and benefits the base stealer.

These factors are addressed in detail in the chapter on base stealing.

Runners in Scoring Position

Learning to hit with men in scoring position is an art. Major-league players are paid huge sums for their ability to drive in runs. We track QAB percentage with men in scoring position by putting a star in the respective box on the quality at-bat chart when runners are in scoring position. The batter's goal is to achieve one of the eight types of quality at-bats with a man in scoring position. A hitter who achieves one of the eight QABs in an RBI situation would be given credit for a productive at-bat regardless of whether he drove in the runner. For example, a batter who draws a walk because he got pitched around would be given a plus for a quality at-bat even though he is not credited with an RBI. Giving a hitter credit for a productive at-bat like drawing a walk in an RBI situation can help facilitate strike-zone discipline. A hitter can only take what the pitcher is willing to give him, and that might mean taking a walk and letting the next batter collect the RBI. Mike Schmidt advised players, "Do less, not more, with runners in scoring position." Emphasizing quality at-bats in RBI situations alleviates stress on the batter because he has options beyond driving in the run to be a productive player. The goal in this category is to be above 50% QABs with runners in scoring position.

Hitters are pitched differently in RBI situations because the pitcher knows that if he gives up a base hit, a run could result. Getting runners on base is one thing; driving them in is another thing entirely. A different approach is in order when it comes to driving in runs as opposed to trying to get on base or moving runners along. Former major leaguer Steve Springer said, "The first pitch with a runner in scoring position will be an off-speed pitch 80% of the time." Hitters have to be proficient at hitting off-speed pitches if they are going to drive in runs. An offense that is skilled at getting runners on base and moving them along will fall short of the seven-run goal if they cannot get runners in. Batters need to practice and master five primary RBI situations:

1. Runner on second base, no outs
2. Runner on second base, two outs
3. Runner on third base, infield back
4. Runner on third base, infield in
5. Bases loaded, less than two outs

Each of these RBI opportunities presents a unique situation in which a batter must be proficient to be a productive offensive player with runners in scoring position. The how-to section that goes into more detail about these five situations is in chapter 10.

Two-Strike Quality At-Bats

According to Felber's research in *The Book on the Book*, a major-league hitter will bat with two strikes on him 49% of the time. My own research on the 2008 College World Series confirms that fact; batters had two strikes on them 48% of the time. The ability of an offense to get a two-strike base hit in that CWS was the number one predictor of a big inning. The average two-strike quality at-bat percentage for teams at the 2008 CWS was 37%. We want batters to have an overall QAB percentage of at least 50%, but quantifying two-strike QAB percentage is critical for realistic performance. To achieve a 50% overall QAB percentage, a hitter would typically have to average 63%

QABs with less than two strikes and 37% QABs with two strikes to break even because he hits with two strikes 50% of the time. Variances from these norms could be red flags that should be addressed.

The 37% QAB percentage with two strikes is a standard by which we can measure players, knowing that players are not going carry as high an average with two strikes as they do with less than two strikes, but they can be productive even when they don't get a base hit. For example, the batter who can move a runner from second to third with a routine ground ball with no outs or collect an RBI with a weak ground ball with the runner at third and the infield back with two strikes has had a productive at-bat even though he did not record a base hit. "Do not strike out with men in scoring position with less than two outs. You are throwing RBIs away," according to Springer.

Two-strike hitting is critical for several reasons:

1. It occurs 50% of the time.
2. It is the number one predictor of a big inning.
3. The pitch count escalates for the opposing pitcher when the batters are not afraid of getting two strikes on them.
4. Critical RBIs can be recorded just by putting the ball in play.
5. It sustains rallies.
6. It frustrates opponents.

Hall of Famer Tony Gwynn said, "Great hitters don't fear hitting with two strikes."

Chase Percentage

Strike-zone awareness is critical to a high-scoring offense. The most famous player in the game, Babe Ruth, made the simple yet profound observation, "Don't swing at almost strikes." The toughest team to pitch to is a team that can hit but is equally skilled at not chasing pitches outside the strike zone. Teams that can hit but chase pitches are vulnerable because pitchers know that they do not have to throw strikes because of the batters' overaggressiveness. This overaggressiveness can lead to both weakly hit balls off the sweet spot of the bat or lots of swings and misses in critical RBI situations. According to famed Oklahoma State coach Gary Ward,

> The greatest hitting situation you can be in is ball one, ball two, ball three. We know statistically that the percentages go up as balls are taken. So the worst thing that could happen is to see a hitter chase the zone.

Strike-zone awareness can create pressure because it forces the opposing pitcher to throw strikes, and quality strikes for that matter, to entice the batter to swing the bat. Wade Boggs, another Hall of Fame player, describing his strike-zone discipline said, "My hitting zone is tighter than the strike zone." If the pitcher is scared of the bats of a great hitting team and they do not chase borderline strikes, then the pitcher's pitch count will elevate quickly and cause his early exit from the game. The game was designed for batters to swing at pitches that they can handle within the strike zone and to take pitches that are either outside the strike zone or are pitchers' pitches.

Productive offensive players understand that a strike is better than an out, meaning that not every strike is a good pitch to hit. One way to track your offense's ability to demonstrate strike-zone discipline is to track how many times during the course of the game they chase pitches outside the strike zone. Bobo Brayton, Hall of Fame coach from the University of Washington, said that if the offense chases more than seven pitches outside the strike zone, it is susceptible to losing the ballgame. During the 2008 College World Series, the University of Miami, which many considered the best offensive club at the CWS that year, chased only 8% percent of pitches outside the strike zone. That statistic is impressive, especially taking into account that the UM batters were facing the best pitchers in the country. To put this in perspective, the average major-league batter chases (swings at pitches outside the strike zone) 21% of the time. These numbers provide the player and coach with benchmarks for training.

Leadoff Man Reaching Base

As previously stated, in Major League Baseball when the leadoff man reaches base, the team has a 95% chance of scoring in that inning. But if the leadoff batter fails to reach base, the team has only a 30% chance of scoring. Our goal for a nine-inning ballgame is for the leadoff man to reach base successfully six out of nine innings, or 67% of the time. Obviously, when the offense can get the leadoff man on base, it has positioned itself favorably to score at least a run in that inning and puts itself in a situation to achieve a big inning. Each batter in the lineup needs to be proficient at being a leadoff man when the opportunity presents itself. One strategy is to tell the batter that he can swing at a first-pitch fastball in his zone. If after the first pitch the count is one ball and no strikes, he must look at the third-base coach for a sign. The coach may give him the green light to swing or the take sign. Both can be advantageous depending on the skills of the batter and the pitcher's stuff. For instance, in MLB the on-base percentage is 100 points better in a 1-0 count versus an 0-1 count, which is significant if the batter's goal is simply to get on base. A batter will hit approximately 25 points better in a 1-0 count versus an 0-1 count. Coaches may need to dictate a hitter's at-bat in certain situations. Guiding batters in a leadoff situation is one of those, especially if the hitter has poor strike-zone discipline.

Pitch Counts

Inducing the opposing team's pitching staff to throw more than 150 pitches in a nine-inning contest has proved to be an important ingredient for the high-scoring offense to secure seven runs. Note that on defense one of our goals is for the pitching staff to throw fewer than 150 pitches during a nine-inning ballgame. During the 2008 College World Series, eventual national champion Fresno State played seven games and threw fewer than 150 pitches five times. Fresno State emerged victorious in those five games, but lost the two games in which they exceeded 150 pitches. By throwing an average of 16 or fewer pitches per inning, Bulldogs starting pitchers were able to throw deep into games. On average, the benchmark for a starting pitcher to remain effective is 100 or fewer pitches. After reaching 100 pitches, most pitchers begin to experience fatigue, which negatively affects their command and velocity. That being said, the sooner the starting pitcher reaches 100 pitches in a game, the sooner he becomes vulnerable. An offense can then force the opponent to go to the bullpen early.

Typically, in college and high school baseball the starting pitcher is better than the bullpen pitchers. If an offense can force the pitcher to throw an average of 20 pitches per inning for five straight innings, he would reach the magical threshold number in the fifth inning. If the starter goes five innings as opposed to seven, the offense would face a pitcher of lesser caliber in the sixth through eighth innings and therefore would have a greater chance to score more runs.

This methodical team approach works well versus pitchers with questionable control. One way to try to drive up pitch counts is to track how many five-pitch at-bats your players have during the game. In Major League Baseball the average batter sees approximately 3.75 pitches per at-bat, so the batter who can see five pitches per at-bat is certainly better than average. If the offense sees five pitches per at-bat on average, they are well on their way to driving the pitcher's pitch count up and sending him to an early shower.

3-to-8

When it comes to offensive pressure, one of the markers of a high-production offense is the ability to hit the ball hard consistently. A great way to measure hard ball contact is the 3-to-8 scale (see figure 3.3). During a contest, we chart every ball put in play by assigning it a number from 0 to 10. A strikeout earns a 0. The goal for the batter is to hit the ball hard on the ground (3), on a line (4-7), or a deep fly ball (8). The team goal heading into a game is 50% or better hard ball contact. Ernie Rosseau, former head baseball coach at Brevard Community College (Florida), would say, "3-to-8 and you'll be great." The harder and flatter the batter impacts the ball, the less reaction time and range the defense has on ground balls, line drives, and fly balls.

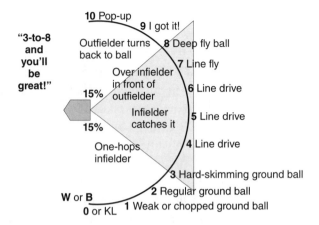

Figure 3.3 3-to-8 scale.

A simple way to gauge weak ground balls is to use the dirt circle in front of home plate. Almost all ground balls that hit the dirt around home plate first are big-hop ground balls and would be scored a 1 or 2. Big-hop ground balls typically result in outs because they are indicative of a mis-hit (not square on the barrel) and bounce up, providing infielders with time to intercept the ball and make the play. A ground ball that strikes the grass first and is hit firmly would be scored a three. For example, if our leadoff batter hits a ground ball to the shortstop, who picks up the ball and throws him out at first, it would be scored as a 6-3 putout, but we would put a small number above the 6-3 that would indicate how hard the ball was hit. If the batter hits a hard ground ball, the person keeping the chart would record the ground ball as a 3. Anyone who looks at the chart after the game can get more information on the quality of the at-bat by noting the hard ball contact score.

Baseball is an unfair game in that a hard line drive can result in an out but a weakly hit ball can fall in for a base hit. The hard ball contact scoring system rewards hitters with a quality at-bat for hitting the ball hard. The odds favor the batter who strikes the ball firmly and consistently on the sweet spot. Over time, his batting average will reflect that. But in high school and fall baseball in college where plate appearances are limited and batting averages can be deceiving, the hard ball contact system paints a more accurate picture of who the better hitters are.

Walks and Hit-by-Pitches

Baseball purists consider a walk the second greatest offensive play in baseball because it is indefensible. "Walks help your team win. One hundred walks is like 100 hits," said major leaguer Ryan Klesko. The home run is clearly the greatest offensive play because it is an instant run (or more) and cannot be defended. Any other ball that is put in play can be defended with proper defensive alignment. Again, walks and hit-by-pitches are critical because they are the building blocks of the big inning. Such seemingly insignificant events are usually the catalyst for the big inning.

Convincing players to appreciate the importance of the walk as a means to reaching base can be a monumental challenge for coaches.

When Gary Ward was the head coach of Oklahoma State for 19 seasons, his teams led all NCAA Division I teams in run production six times, including four consecutive years from 1985 through 1988. During those 19 years his teams averaged 9.2 runs per game. And what fueled that incredible run production was a remarkable on-base percentage by his hitters, which was kick-started by walks. Breaking it down further, his teams walked more than any team in NCAA Division I history, which allowed the on-base percentage to shoot through the roof. Over 19 years at Oklahoma State, his teams averaged 7.1 walks per game. In 15 of those 19 seasons, his batters walked at least 415 times per season, and reached a maximum of 607 walks during the 1986 season. That year OSU batters walked an average of 8.5 times per game. "It isn't about taking pitches," says Ward. "A lot of people get confused about going out and taking a bunch of pitches. The reality is that you must value being disciplined at the plate" (Pavlovich).

When the pitcher is struggling to throw strikes, the batter should just let the pitcher hang himself and not panic by swinging at pitches outside the strike zone. High-scoring offenses also accumulate a lot of hit-by-pitches because hitters hold their ground. These batters know how to move out of the way of a pitch with proper hitting mechanics. They roll back toward the catcher, drop the bat, and tuck the head, maintaining their position in the batter's box, which will lead to more HBPs and a free pass to first.

Game goals are critical for the high-scoring offense because they provide direction. Don Shula, the winningest coach in NFL history, has stated that every team needs to have a goalpost to kick at, meaning that every team needs to know exactly what they're trying to do before every game. Having well-defined, clear goals helps a team stay focused. Players are able to focus on achieving the game goals and playing against the game rather than worrying about their opponent.

Stealing bases, moving runners, exercising strike-zone discipline, and understanding the importance of having the leadoff man reach base are all components of a high-scoring offense. An offense that is attacking and dictating the tempo of the game is an offense that will cause the defense to make mistakes. Forcing the defense to play at a faster pace often creates mistakes. The offense that accumulates free bases in the form of walks and HBPs increases their odds of obtaining a big inning and, ultimately, achieving seven runs.

PART II

Run Production

Scoring runs was, in the new view, less an art or talent than a process. If you made the process as routine—if you've got every player doing his part on the production line—you could pay a lot less for runs than the going rate.

Michael Lewis, Moneyball

Grinding out quality at-bats, such as bunts that are well-placed, eight-pitch at-bats, collecting RBIs, moving runners, and having strike zone awareness, are all skills of a productive offensive player that contribute to run production. Run production is more than nine talented players trying to get a base hit and hoping they can string three hits together in a single inning to outscore their opponent. Rather, a proficient offense that is consistent is a team made up of nine players who are unselfish and pass the baton of a quality at-bat on to the next hitter in order to form a strong chain, held together by a mental and physical strategy for success. The offense understands that competing in the batter's box is only half of the battle, but aggressive and intelligent base running is what scores runs.

CHAPTER 4

Defining a Quality At-Bat

Do not think about your batting average. It's about quality at-bats.

Steve Springer, former major-league player and author of *Quality At-Bats* audio CD

Many baseball purists think that a great offensive player is one who can hit, but most high school, college, and even professional teams have few pure hitters. As a result, a high-scoring offense needs to have a system wherein players who do not hit for average are able to contribute to the offense in ways other than just swinging the bat.

PRODUCTIVE OFFENSIVE PLAYERS

Baseball is a game of failure. A typical big-league hitter's batting average is around .267, which means that he fails more than 70% of the time. With failure occurring at such a high rate, crediting hitters for productive at-bats, not simply hits, helps their confidence and makes the offense function better as a unit. "Production is the key word," according to hitting guru Steve Springer. For example, moving a runner from second to third with no outs by hitting a ground ball to the right side will help your team because the runner can then score without the aid of a base hit. When coaches and teammates positively acknowledge hitters for these kinds of productive outs, hitters are free to be less concerned with their batting average and can instead focus on helping the offense score runs. Players gain confidence when they are credited for helping the offense be productive even when they are not collecting base hits. In a survey of big-league players who were asked what baseball skill they most desired, they answered, "Confidence." This sentiment is summarized well by Springer, who said, "Have enough quality ABs and try to drive the baseball. That's all you can do. Confidence every single day, every single AB." Anything coaches can do to build players' confidence has an incredible effect on their ability to perform a task as difficult as hitting a baseball.

Successful offensive players are those who help the team score runs, bottom line. A team's ability to score runs depends more on the accumulation of quality at-bats than a bunch of individual high batting averages. A person's batting average tells only a small part of the story of that player's offensive production. "Batting average needs companion statistics to better describe a player's contribution to his team. There are other numbers that are better storytellers than RBI, home runs, or batting average" (Keri, 2006). Productive offensive players value quality at-bats.

Eight Ways to Get a Quality At-Bat

Clearly defining for players exactly what a quality at-bat is helps them understand clearly how they can contribute to the offense. Our program has identified eight ways to earn a quality at-bat:

1. Base hit
2. Hit a ball hard (see 3-to-8 chart in chapter 3)
3. Walk

4. HBP

5. RBI

6. Well-placed bunt

7. Over and in (with no outs, move runner from second base to third base)

8. Eight-pitch at-bat

The bull's-eye graphic in figure 4.1 illustrates the various ways that a hitter can achieve one of the eight quality at-bats. At its center is the hitter's ultimate goal of achieving a quality at-bat. Beginning at the outermost ring and moving inward toward the QAB goal, the actions that result in a quality at-bat increase in difficulty. In ring one, strike-zone discipline, a hitter does not even have to put the ball in play to have a quality at-bat. Simply exercising strike-zone discipline and drawing a walk, being hit by a pitch, or fouling off pitches to force an eight-pitch at-bat is sufficient to reach the goal.

Figure 4.1 Quality at-bat bull's-eye.

The second ring, bunting, requires some bat-control skill but does not ask a hitter to reach base. Ring three, situational hitting, asks for a higher level of bat control and requires a purposeful approach to move a runner but still does not require a batter to reach base safely. The fourth ring, base hit, asks the batter to reach base and to adjust his mental approach to the at-bat based on the count. Ring five demands that a batter not only put the ball in play but bring a runner home. Hitting a hard line drive with backspin is the most difficult thing for a hitter to do, but it is also the most productive at-bat, which is why 3-to-8 hard contact is closest to the bull's-eye. A hard line drive can result in anything from a home run to a lineout, but odds are that the back-spun line drive will have a positive effect on the offense. In reality, a batter can accomplish several of the target objectives in any given at-bat, such as fouling off pitches to get an eight-pitch at-bat and then hitting a line drive with the bases loaded and recording two RBIs. For purposes of charting, however, the batter is credited with having one quality at-bat.

As stated earlier, the game of baseball is unfair. For instance, a batter may hit a hard line drive right at the shortstop. The ball is caught, and the player is penalized because his batting average goes down. Many productive offensive plays that batters accomplish are not recorded as base hits and, therefore, do not boost their batting averages. Giving batters credit for quality at-bats not only boosts their confidence but also increases their willingness to do what it takes to help the ballclub score runs. Changing a batter's focus from trying to get a base hit to getting a quality at-bat is an important step for players to take as they transition from trying to be a great hitter, of which few are capable, and instead doing what it takes to be a productive offensive player. Every player must understand that probably only two or three batters on the team can hit for a high average. The rest of the lineup needs to have other ways to contribute to the offense besides getting a base hit. If a player is rewarded only when he records a base hit, then he will feel like a failure 70% of the time, which may devastate his confidence level. Seven of the eight quality at-bats do not include producing a base hit.

Stringing Together Quality At-Bats

Achieving a quality at-bat is the goal for the individual hitter, but it is the ability of the nine-man lineup to string together five or more quality at-bats that is the key to producing a big inning. Individual QABs mean little if they do not come in bunches. For example, a batter gets a quality at-bat and reaches first base, that goes for naught if the next batter rolls over into a double play. The result would be two outs and nobody on base. The next batter gets a base hit, but that is followed by a weak pop-up. At the conclusion of the inning the quality at-bat chart would show two QABs out of four plate appearances, 50% QABs, but no runs because the offense could not string them together. The cycle was broken by one bad at-bat, which stymied any hope for a big inning.

Stringing together quality at-bats is like assembling a giant chain that is only as strong as its weakest link. Many would-be productive innings have been ended by a batter striking out looking or hooking a ground ball that results in an inning-ending double play. Getting quality at-bats is critical, but stringing them together collectively is what produces results on the scoreboard. Nothing is more exciting in baseball than a rally that develops because players are working together and grinding out quality at-bats. The QAB chart we use has a column marked "String," which refers to the ability of the offense to produce quality at-bats consecutively, one after another, to assemble a strong, uninterrupted chain. This chart is discussed in more detail in chapter 12. Research indicates that stringing together five or more quality at-bats can produce a big inning at least 40% of the time.

A Closer Look at QABs

Looking a little deeper into quality at-bats, segmenting them into categories such as at-bats with two strikes and those with less than two strikes, makes sense, because both occur approximately 50% of the time. The eight-team field at the 2008 College World Series produced a quality at-bat percentage with two strikes at a 37% rate. This figure serves as a benchmark for good teams when batters have two strikes on them. Statistically speaking, when batters get two strikes on them they will not be as productive. For example, if your team is average with two strikes, they will have a 37% QAB percentage, which encompasses about half of their at-bats. To get the team percentage up to 50%, the team would need to be 63% with less than two strikes, which represents the other half of the team at-bats. Perfecting the art of two-strike hitting is critical for the high-scoring offense because it extends innings, moves runners, and leads to big innings.

The two greatest plays in baseball are the home run and the walk because both are indefensible. The third greatest play is fouling off a two-strike pitch because it could lead to the second greatest play: the walk. One of the benefits of tracking quality at-bat percentage with two strikes and less than two strikes is that it identifies for players and coaches which 50% they need to spend more time on.

Another important statistic that bears a closer look is how often batters have a quality at-bat with runners in scoring position. In approximately 25% of the at-bats during a game, runners will be in scoring position. Tracking quality at-bats with runners in scoring position provides feedback for players and coaches on how productive batters are in critical RBI situations. For example, a quality at-bat percentage with runners in scoring position under 50% would indicate a deficiency in that area. In Major League Baseball telecasts, you often see a graphic that shows a player's batting average with men in scoring position. If a player has a high average with runners in scoring position, he probably makes a lot of money. Batting average with men in scoring position tells only part of the story. Players should be rewarded for drawing walks and moving runners when guys are in scoring position. In amateur baseball not everyone is a proficient hitter, and drawing a walk is sometimes just as important as driving in the run. Coaches need to recognize those occasions when a batter is being pitched around does not chase pitches and instead takes his walk. If players know that coaches are giving players credit for a walk with men in scoring position, they will be less anxious and be less apt to chase pitches out of the zone. Taking a closer look at what actually occurs in RBI situations can be revealing. Patterns such as striking out looking and chasing pitches outside the strike zone can be identified and corrected. When a player produces a quality at-bat when a runner is in scoring position, the coach can place a star on the quality at-bat chart in the player's box. When the game is over, these marks can be tallied to come up with a cumulative QAB percentage for the game.

PITCHER VERSUS HITTER CONFRONTATION

The battle that takes place between the pitcher and hitter in baseball is the front line, where the critical combat in the game takes place. The outcome of the confrontation between the pitcher and hitter determines most of the

Texas Rangers Model

At the major-league level the Texas Rangers employ a similar quality at-bat system. They call it the Texas Rangers' productive team plate appearance system. The Rangers' system includes eight ways of collecting a positive at-bat:

1. Hit
2. Walk
3. Hit-by-pitch or catcher interference
4. Sacrifice fly
5. Sacrifice bunt
6. Advance lead runner with an out
7. Advance lead runner by an error
8. Eight-pitch at-bat

The Texas Rangers team goal is to collect 17 productive plate appearances in the course of a nine-inning game. This system, fostered by hitting coach Clint Hurdle for the 2010 Texas Rangers, helped guide them to the 2010 playoffs. Their motto was "Let's find a way to get there every game."

Whether at the Little League, Babe Ruth, high school, college, or professional level, a system that employs quality at-bats has proven effective when it comes to scoring runs above the league average. The eight ways that we have defined quality at-bats differ subtly from what the Texas Rangers defined as productive at-bats. The main point is to implement a system that clearly defines a quality at-bat and emphasizes that stringing them together leads to a big inning. Whether the goal is 17 for the game or 50% for the game, the accumulation of QABs is a proven predictor of a high-scoring offense. Establishing clear definitions for productive at-bats and game goals allows players to be evaluated fairly and consistently, not only on a game-by-game basis but over the course of a long season.

offensive production of that particular inning. Baseball is a team game mixed with periods of one-on-one confrontations that take place approximately 40 times, on both offense and defense, in a nine-inning ballgame. We ask the batter to win 50% of those confrontations by producing a quality at-bat. Although hitting a baseball may be the most difficult task in all of sport, equipping hitters with skills besides just swinging the bat increases their productivity. The one fact that every team knows is that when the game starts the offense has 27 outs to work with.

Typically, in a nine-inning ballgame an offensive team will have at least 40 plate appearances, 40 opportunities to achieve a quality at-bat. The pitcher's goal is to get the batter out in as few pitches as possible and ultimately to record three outs before the offense scores a run. On the other hand, the batter wants to get a quality at-bat, and the offense wants to score as many runs as possible before the defense records three outs. Hence, the battle for supremacy starts and ends with the pitcher versus batter confrontation, all within a space of 60 feet, 6 inches (18.4 m). It starts for the offense at the plate. The battle must be won on the front line.

2008 College World Series

An analysis of data from the 2008 NCAA Division I men's College World Series can help us understand how important quality at-bats are to scoring runs and winning baseball games. The Bulldogs of Fresno State, the eventual national champion in 2008, won five games and lost two during the World Series. In the five games that they won, the Bulldogs had two things in common. First, in all five wins, they achieved at least 50% or better quality at-bats on the offensive side of the ledger. Pitching, of course, is critical, and in four of those five wins the Bulldogs' pitching staff threw fewer than 150 pitches. In the two games that they lost their quality at-bat percentage was below 50%, although the pitchers threw fewer than 150 pitches in one of those two losses.

Does the high-scoring offensive model work at the elite Division I level? It has been successful at the college programs that I have been associated with, but does it translate outside our program? We've seen that the Texas Rangers have used a similar system, one that defines a productive plate appearance and a definite game goal. I charted all 17 games of the 2008 NCAA Division I College World Series and inserted the data into grade cards for all eight teams. The high-scoring model produced some interesting results.

The quality at-bat percentage of all eight teams at the 2008 CWS was 51%. We took a closer look at the batters' ability to achieve a quality at-bat with less than two strikes, which they did at a 63% rate. When the hitters had two strikes on them, they achieved a quality at-bat only 37% of the time. At the major-league level, hitters have two strikes on them 49% of the time, and in the 2008 CWS batters had two strikes on them 48% of the time. To achieve the goal of a 50% quality at-bat percentage overall, hitters need to have a quality at-bat percentage of 63% with less than two strikes and 37% or better with two strikes. Dissecting quality at-bats into two parts is extremely helpful when evaluating players. By breaking down the numbers, players and coaches will be able to see whether individual players have a weakness with less than two strikes or with two strikes and then make the necessary adjustments.

THE COUNT

The count plays an important role in determining whether the hitter achieves a quality at-bat. "It is central to the question of situational batting success because the count is the leverage the batter and pitcher wield against one another in the fight for dominance at the plate" (Felber, 2005, p. 29).

Table 4.1 shows that a batter has almost a 60% chance of achieving a quality at-bat in the first two pitches. Contrast that with what happens when the batter has two strikes on him; he has roughly a 28% chance of getting a quality at-bat excluding a 3-2 count, which many do not consider a true two-strike count. What does all this data mean? One of the important conclusions is the importance of hitting with the count in the batter's favor. Moreover, the 0-0 count, the 0-1 count, and the 1-0 count are virtually the same in terms of the hitter's ability to obtain a QAB. The batter who has an 0-2 count or a 1-2 count really has to battle and shorten his stroke to achieve a quality at-bat because the odds are stacked against him. One of the most interesting things about tracking quality at-bats in comparison to the count is realizing that the batter who finds himself with any three-ball count will achieve a quality at-bat 74% of the time. So if a batter gets two strikes on him but can fight his way to a three-ball count, he is likely to achieve a productive at-bat. On the other side of the coin, pitchers must try to avoid three-ball counts at all costs.

This information can be useful in teaching players the importance of being aggressive early in the count with runners in scoring position. This data show that having a productive plate appearance in an 0-2, 1-2, or 2-2 count is highly unlikely. The data also indicate that with two strikes an average batter has a quality at-bat 37% of the time. A hitter's ability to obtain a productive plate appearance is directly linked to the count.

Table 4.1 Quality At-Bat Percentage Based on Count

Action	0-0 5,000 ABs	0-1	1-0 348 action	1-1	2-0 136 action	2-1	3-0	3-1	0-2	1-2	2-2	3-2
QAB% 51%	58%	62%	59%	50%	64%	57%	97%	88%	25%	26%	32%	62%

Three-ball counts			Less than two strikes			With two strikes		
QAB%	206/280	74%	QAB%	432/684	63%	QAB%	233/627	37%

Motivation Through Recognition

In football, especially high school and college, individual players often earn award decals for exceptional play. In 2008 the Fresno State baseball coaching staff awarded helmet decals to batters for executing the team's offensive system. Rewarding players with helmet stickers (figure 4.2) is a good way to reinforce or give hitters credit for quality at-bats. Anything that coaches can do to reward players for executing the offensive system can prove to be productive for the team. Here are some examples of ways that coaches can recognize their players for executing on offense.

Figure 4.2 Batting helmet decals are awarded after each game for executing the offensive system.

1. Leadoff batter reaching base safely
2. Player who earns a freebie and ultimately scores a run
3. Two-strike at-bat resulting in getting on base, moving runner from second base to third base with no outs
4. RBI
5. Perfect day (at least three quality at-bats in a row)

The building block of a high-scoring offense is the quality at-bat. Each player's goal when he comes to the plate is to achieve one of the eight quality at-bats and pass the torch to the guy on deck. Each at-bat is linked to the next, thereby creating a chain. The chain becomes strong when five batters in a row collect quality at-bats. Stringing together at least five quality at-bats one time during a game is an absolute in creating a big inning. The accumulation of quality at-bats and stringing them together is the formula for a high-scoring offense.

Having eight ways to have a positive effect on the offense is important because players realize that they can contribute in other ways besides getting a base hit or collecting an RBI. According to Steve Springer,

> They should throw away the BA in the minors. It doesn't teach a person to fail and still be confident. There should be a quality AB champion. One is a sac fly, two is get the guy over, three is hit the ball hard. That's all you can do.

With failure being so prominent in the game, especially in terms of hitting, providing hitters with alternatives to the base hit does wonders for their psyche.

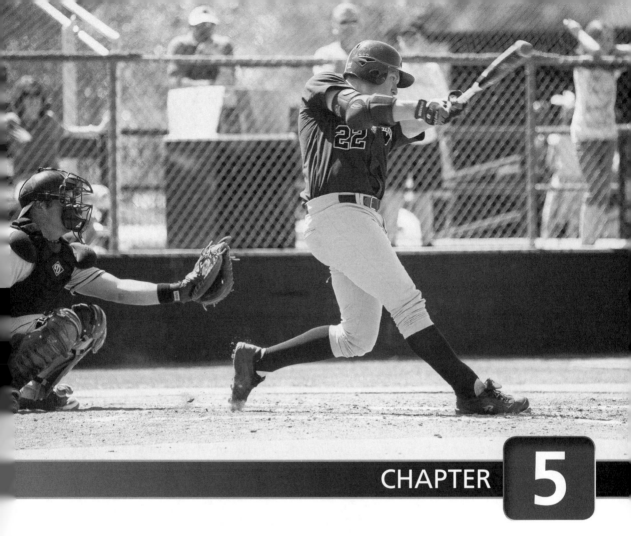

CHAPTER 5

The Ultimate Hitter

Every time I stepped into the box with a bat in my hand, I felt sorry for the pitcher.

Rogers Hornsby, Hall of Fame major-league infielder

W hat does the ultimate productive hitter look like? The ultimate hitter can hit hard backspin line drives consistently from foul line to foul line. He possesses great bat speed, is aggressive on hitters' pitches, and is able to lay off pitchers' pitches. He is poised in the batter's box. He is in control of the at-bat, not the pitcher. He is extremely balanced and has a plan when he steps into the box. When he takes a pitch, he tracks the ball with his head all the way back to the catcher. He maintains balance with good hitting posture from start to finish. The ball jumps off his bat, and he always takes his best swing; he does not take off-balance swings and is not fooled with less than two strikes. He can make pitch-by-pitch adjustments based on what the pitcher has thrown. He adjusts to the situation and is able to fine-tune his timing. The ultimate hitter has great energy, meaning that he transfers his weight properly throughout the swing. He has what we call relaxed bat speed and controlled momentum.

Now that the characteristics of the ultimate hitter have been defined, the challenge becomes training those characteristics in each player so that they positively affect the overall offensive scheme. Hitting may be the most difficult skill in all of sport. Numerous books have been written on the mechanics of the swing, the mental side of hitting, and mastering the swing. The purpose of this section is to focus on the areas that make up an outstanding hitter, simplify the process, and train the characteristics of the ultimate hitter to make him the cornerstone of a high-scoring offense.

THE GOAL IN HITTING

No discussion on hitting can begin unless we understand what the goal in hitting is. In a camp setting, for example, when we ask campers what they are trying to do when they are at the plate, they typically respond, "I'm trying to get a base hit." We explain that getting a base hit is out of the hitter's control. In fact, the only sure base hit is a ball that goes over the fence, because the defense cannot catch that ball. For that reason, the home run is the greatest offensive play: It is indefensible and results in an instant run. When asked what the goal is in basketball, most young players respond that it is to put the ball in the hoop to score points for their team. The goal in hitting, as defined by Ernie Rosseau, former head coach of Brevard Community College (Florida), is to hit hard backspin line drives consistently off the sweet spot of the bat. Again, the goal is not to get a base hit because the outcome is out of the batter's control.

Rosseau's definition is the foundation for the ultimate productive hitter and the high-scoring offense. Line drives give the hitter the greatest chance to get a base hit because line drives reduce the reaction time of the defense. Training must always be focused on hitting hard backspin line drives consistently. Of course, during the game a ground ball can move a runner or score a run, as can a fly ball, but a line-drive stroke is the foundation. Learning to manipulate the club head to create a line drive down or a line drive up is easier after a flat line-drive stroke is in place.

With the implementation of the BBCOR (batted ball coefficient of restitution) bat in 2011 at the college level and in 2012 at the high school level, the game has changed dramatically. *NCAA Division I Baseball Statistics Trends (1970-2011)* illustrates the reduction in offensive productivity. For example, in 2011 batting average was down 23 points, run scoring dropped by nearly 1.5 runs per game, and home runs fell off by nearly 40% from the previous year.

These new bats act more like wood bats. They have a smaller sweet spot and diminished ball exit speed. A hitter must be more precise in his stroke because the bat is less forgiving with the smaller sweet spot. In addition, the weight distribution is different, which increases the difficulty of controlling the barrel and requires greater balance and a better fundamental stroke. The goal in hitting remains the same, but swinging effectively with the new bats requires a more precise stroke.

Table 5.1   NCAA Division I Baseball Statistics, 2010 and 2011

	Teams	Batting average	Runs per game	Home runs per game
2010	292	.305	6.98	0.94
2011 (BBCOR)	292	.282	5.58	0.52

Data from NCAA, 2011, *NCAA Division I baseball records*. [Online]. Available://fs.ncaa.org/Docs/stats/baseball_RB/2012/D1.pdf [October 17, 2012].

PROPER APPROACH

Hitters spend a tremendous amount of time on their stroke development. Although this work is important, it is about third on my list when it comes to what makes an effective hitter. We have all seen players with great swings who are not productive because their timing is incorrect or their approach is bad. Proper timing would be second for me in importance when defining what makes a great hitter.

Top Three Priorities of an Effective Hitter

1. Approach
2. Timing
3. Mechanics

We have seen players who have imperfect mechanics but still have a knack for arriving on time. They hit better in games than teammates who have better swings but allow pitchers to disrupt their timing. The best hitters have the best approach, and they have a mental and physical strategy for success before they step into the batter's box. "You don't have to leave it all up to chance. Good hitters don't just go up and swing. They always have a plan," according to Hall of Fame player Dave Winfield. "Call it an educated deduction. You visualize. You're like a good negotiator. You know what you have, you know what he has, and then you try to work it out."

Steve Springer said his approach was, "Sit on what you are going to get up in the zone and attack the inside part of the baseball." Most hitters want the fastball, so they sit fastball every pitch. The problem with that approach is that at the higher levels the pitchers have command of their secondary pitches (curveballs and changeups). To be effective, hitters must be ready and willing to hit off-speed pitches. Hitters must also understand that a strike is better than an out. Taking a fastball for a strike at your knees on the outside corner of the plate early in the count is OK. If the hitter swings at this pitch, he could easily make an out. All strikes are not good pitches to hit. The ultimate hitter wants strikes that are in his power zone, which for most players means balls that are up in the strike zone. Attacking the inside part of the ball helps ensure that the hitter stays on the ball, affording him the opportunity to drive the ball from foul line to foul line as he approaches the ball from the inside out and stays long through the baseball. Although Springer's approach is simple, players may struggle with this methodology because many cannot get past anticipating a fastball on every pitch.

Other approaches to hitting are sound as well. For example, Mike Schmidt said that when he was at the plate he tried to hit a line drive off the pitcher's knees. He thought that his approach helped him stay through the middle of the field, with a line-drive down stroke, so that he would not lift the ball. The Oakland Athletics have a sound approach as well, saying simply, "Cover high." This notion has the hitter anticipating every pitch to be up in the zone

Practice Tip

Coaches should have the pitcher change speeds in batting practice and not let the hitters know what is coming. The BP pitcher should throw curveballs and changeups; simply throwing a BP fastball for every pitch doesn't simulate a game. Mixing up pitches replicates what hitters will see in a real game and, ultimately, forces them to focus and make adjustments. What coaches are really hoping for is that players hit hanging breaking balls that are up in the zone, take off-speed pitches that are below the zone, and arrive on time on fastballs away.

so that he is always attacking down on the baseball and never working up to hit. Having the right approach is the most important ingredient for the ultimate hitter, but it is the most difficult attribute to master.

UP THE MIDDLE: UTM

Hitting the baseball through the middle two-thirds of the field allows the hitter to stay on more pitches, provides the greatest opportunity for extra-base hits, and allows the most opening for an error. At some point in their careers, most hitters are told to hit the ball up the middle. But either consciously or subconsciously, they find themselves pulling the ball or trying to carve the ball to the back side of the field.

The game of baseball is all about failure. We want to stay away from extremes, from the six hole to the third-base foul line and from the four hole to the first-base foul line. A ball hit firm and flat into those areas will most likely be a hit, but we want the attitude that these events result from a flat swing that is either slightly early or slightly late and not intentional. In both practice and in games, the batter should be trying to hit the ball from gap to gap. This approach gives the batter the best opportunity to stay away from extremes and helps him avoid rollover ground balls and routine fly balls to the back side of the field.

Former Red Sox standout Mo Vaughn said, "I've got sights when I go up to the plate. In Fenway, I put my sights on that left-center-field wall. I'm looking to aim myself to hit the ball at that spot." To reinforce this concept and help players develop the UTM mind-set, you can place cones from behind the shortstop to the left-center-field gap and from behind the second-base position to the right-center-field gap (figure 5.1). This layout provides players with a clear vision of the middle two-thirds of the field in practice. Although this concept is simple, the spray charts of most hitters and teams would likely show that most balls are hit outside the middle two-thirds. Teams and players who can consistently hit the ball through the middle of field will be more productive than those who cannot.

THE CONTEST FOR CONTROL OF THE BALL

Who is in control of the at-bat? That is the question! The greatest confrontation in baseball is the 60-foot, 6-inch (18.4 m) skirmish that takes place between the hitter and the pitcher. The game starts and ends there, and whoever wins the majority of those skirmishes will likely win the battle. Baseball is unique in that the defense, specifically the pitcher, begins the contest with control of the ball. John Cohen, the head coach at Mississippi State University, described the relationship between a batter and a pitcher, specifically as it relates to control of the at-bat, as a that of a puppet and a puppeteer. The

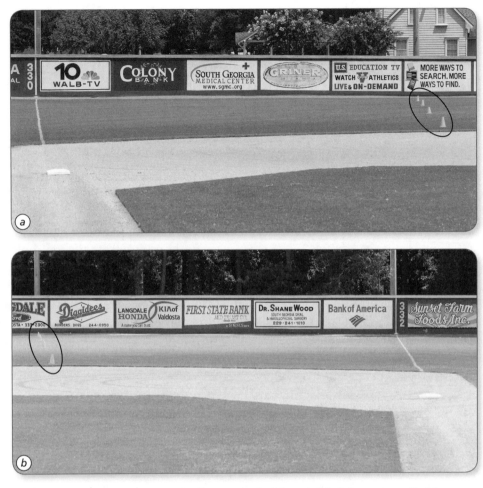

Figure 5.1 Place cones in *(a)* left center field and *(b)* right center field to create a visual of the middle of the field for hitters.

description is certainly accurate. Is the hitter–puppet being directed by the pitcher–puppeteer because he is chasing pitches outside the strike zone? "A hitter's impatience is the pitcher's biggest advantage," said Pete Rose. Or are the roles reversed? Is the batter forcing the pitcher to elevate his pitches? Who is in control of the at-bat?

According to legendary slugger Ted Williams, "A decent hitter can hit a good pitch three times better than a great hitter can hit a bad pitch." The answer is that the ultimate hitter is the puppeteer: He is controlling the at-bat. How does he do that? First, he has a great approach, sitting on what he is going to get up in the strike zone, and he attacks the inside of the baseball. The batter who is in control works the count to his advantage. Opponents fear him because he has incredible plate coverage, great strike-zone discipline, and the ability to make adjustments. The hitter who is the puppeteer is a poised and has great balance that allows him to have maximum bat speed at the point of contact. He can deliver his best swing on off-speed pitches. To be the puppeteer, the hitter must not miss pitches that he can handle when he does get them.

The great former manager of the New York Yankees and Los Angeles Dodgers, Joe Torre, said that during his MVP year he never remembers fouling a ball straight back the entire season. What an incredible achievement—getting your pitch and not missing it! The ultimate hitter has a fundamentally sound swing and great timing but more importantly possesses a great mental and physical strategy that gives him an advantage over the pitcher and helps him dictate the at-bat.

STRIKE-ZONE DISCIPLINE

The New York Yankees have a saying, "You're only as good as the pitch you swing at." This adage is similar to the sage advice of Shoeless Joe Jackson to "get a good pitch to hit." Learning to swing at good pitches starts in practice in all drills in which the ball is put in flight, from front toss to batting practice. Coaches must demand that hitters swing at pitches that they can handle and take pitches that they cannot drive. The book *Moneyball* (Lewis, 2003) caused a stir in the baseball community because it clearly stated that the Oakland Athletics actively sought players who had high on-base percentages and compensated them accordingly. For decades, evaluations of professional baseball players were based solely on the five physical tools, not statistical data such as OBP. The Oakland Athletics went so far as to say that strike-zone discipline was the sixth tool. According to legendary baseball manager Branch Rickey,

> The greatest single difference between a major-league and minor-league batsman is the difference in his judgment of the strike zone. The major leaguer knows better the difference between a ball and a strike. He knows better whether to swing or take a pitch.

Five Physical Tools

1. Hit
2. Hit for power
3. Field
4. Throw
5. Run

The Oakland Athletics have helped shed light on one of the primary functions of a productive hitter, which is simply to get on base and put the offense in position to score runs. Getting a good pitch to hit helps a hitter hit the ball hard consistently, and a hitter who has learned not to swing at borderline pitches will earn more walks. Ted Williams shared some clear and concise wisdom when he said,

> *Nearly every hitter has a certain type pitch in a particular spot in his strike zone which he finds hard to hit. For some, it's high and inside while others have trouble hitting anything that's low and away. On this kind of ball, and if the count is less than two strikes, take the pitch.*

Williams believed that the two best statistics by which to define a hitter were on-base percentage and slugging percentage. Arguing with Mr. Williams' statement is difficult because both getting on base and hitting for power contribute to the ultimate goal of scoring runs. Both hinge on the hitter's ability to hit his pitch, not the pitcher's pitch.

Most hitters and coaches would not deny that strike-zone awareness is important, and both are often frustrated when players chase pitches outside the strike zone and get themselves out. As Johnny Mize once stated, "The pitcher has to throw a strike sooner or later, so why not hit the pitch you want to hit and not the one he wants you to hit?" At the basic level, the strike zone is the essence of the game. The pitcher is trying to put the ball in the lower quadrant of the strike zone, and the hitter is trying to induce the pitcher to throw the ball up in the strike zone. The confrontation is a sophisticated game of cat and mouse between the pitcher and hitter. When the hitter shows the pitcher that he will chase a ball outside the strike zone, the pitcher–puppeteer knows that he does not have to throw that hitter a strike to retire him. Bobo Brayton, the former head baseball coach at the University of Washington and ABCA Hall of Fame inductee, was quoted as saying that if a team chases seven pitches outside the strike zone, they are susceptible to losing. Exceptional hitters and offensive teams understand the importance of controlling the strike zone and work on it diligently (figure 5.2).

Figure 5.2 In batting practice, use a catch net or catcher to delineate the strike zone.

Put a five-gallon paint bucket upside down on home plate during batting practice (figure 5.3). The purpose of the bucket is to deter players from swinging at pitches below their knees, to reinforce the concept of getting a pitch up in the strike zone to hit and taking pitcher's pitches that are down in the zone.

Figure 5.3 A five-gallon bucket reminds players to avoid swinging at pitches below the knees.

ADJUSTMENTS: "ASK LOUE"

The statement holds true that great hitters make adjustments pitch to pitch, good hitters at-bat to at-bat, average hitters game to game, and poor hitters never. Brad Weitzel, assistant baseball coach at the University of Florida, made the comment that dinosaurs are extinct because they could not adapt, could not make adjustments. Hitters who can't make adjustments are dinosaurs who won't be around very long.

Adjustments start in practice when hitters need to learn and gather information from every swing. Hitters need to ask themselves on each swing: Was I *late*? Was I *over* the ball? Was I *under* the ball? Was I *early*? L-O-U-E. These four letters encompass how a hitter swings at pitches and what adjustments he needs to make. Hitters who can make adjustments in batting practice have a better chance of doing this when they step into the batter's box on game day. Kevin Stocker, former shortstop with the St. Louis Cardinals, when asked why he made it to the big leagues so quickly, said, "The coach never had to tell me the same thing twice." Stocker had the ability to adjust quickly and not repeat mistakes. Every hitter needs to adjust. The great ones do it quickly and consistently. At every level of baseball, the hitters who can adjust have longer careers, and those who cannot adjust, the dinosaurs, may see their careers end abruptly. The simple command to "Ask LOUE" is an easy way to evaluate swings in practice. Hitters need to make the correct adjustments quickly and efficiently to be successful.

LESS THAN TWO STRIKES
AND WITH TWO STRIKES

Although hitters can find themselves in twelve possible counts, we simplify our hitting approach into two distinct categories: counts with less than two strikes and counts with two strikes. With less than two strikes, the expectation is to hit the ball hard every time. I asked Ernie Rousseau his opinion on what percentage of the time a hitter should hit the ball hard with less than two strikes. He said a hard hit should occur 100 percent of the time. Although this expectation might be unrealistic, it can certainly serve as the goal with less than two strikes.

After the hitter has two strikes on him, he needs to widen his strike zone and change his mental approach to be "late and on top" to protect against the off-speed pitch. Among the worst things that a hitter can do in a two-strike count are

1. being early,
2. being under, and
3. striking out looking (especially on a pitch on the outer half of the plate).

Percentages tell us that most strikeouts in college baseball occur on balls outside the strike zone. Presumably, that tendency holds true for high school as well. Hitters make the mistake of forgetting Babe Ruth's sage advice not to swing at "almost strikes." Pitchers are counting on hitters to chase pitches outside the strike zone. While playing for the Colorado Rockies, Andres Galarraga was told by the organization that it did not matter if he struck out as long as he struck out on strikes. Strikeouts happen, but they can be minimized with the correct approach. The "late and on top" approach helps the hitter allow the ball to travel deep into the strike zone and facilitates keeping the bat head above the center of the ball, which promotes a short swing. Albert Pujols does not make physical adjustments with two strikes because his swing is mechanically sound. He does, however, change his approach with two strikes by letting the ball travel as deep into the strike zone as possible. This approach allows him more time to recognize pitches and not chase pitches outside the strike zone.

A hitter is always in one of two count scenarios, with less than two strikes and with two strikes, and each occurs about 50% of the time. From a standpoint of quality at-bats, the hitter needs to be at 63% with less than two strikes and at 37% with two strikes to achieve 50% quality at-bats overall.

The proper mental approach is a critical component for the productive hitter, and that approach can and should change based on the count. Again, the focus is on the two fundamental counts—with less than two strikes and with two strikes. Each scenario brings a set of expectations and a specific approach.

Less Than Two Strikes

Approach: "Sit on what you are going to get up in the strike zone and attack the inside part of the baseball."

Truism #1: "If you're fooled, don't fool with it."

Truism #2: "When ahead never late."

Outcome: The batter should hit the ball hard 100% of the time because he is swinging at pitches that he is looking for and taking pitches that are in his power zone. He is always getting his best swing because he is committed to the pitch.

With Two Strikes

Approach: "Late and on top."

Truism #1: "Never strike out on a ball away."

Truism #2: "When behind never early."

Outcome: By letting the ball travel deeper into the strike zone, the hitter is able to fight off tough pitches and might be able to draw a walk. He is also more apt to record a productive out for his team by moving a runner with a ground ball. One of the tenets of championship baseball is the ability of hitters to put the ball in play consistently.

MASTER THESE THREE POSITIONS

From a strictly mechanical standpoint, a productive hitter needs to master three things:

1. **Head position:** In the setup, both eyes are focused on the pitcher (figure 5.4a) and the nose is over the toes for proper balance, not head over heels. The head stays in the center of the body throughout the entire swing (figure 5.4b). The chin is dropped, or nodded, to the ball at contact and remains in that position from impact through extension and follow-through (figure 5.4c). Proper head position facilitates reading the pitch, expanding plate coverage, improving balance, and producing more power.

2. **Lower half:** The lower half has two functions. The first is to put the body in a position to hit (launch), and the second is to generate energy into and through the bat, which we call block and drive.

   a. **Launch:** To get to launch, the hitter must execute proper stride mechanics. Proper stride mechanics can be described as follows:

      Low, slow, and on the toe (front foot)

      Slow, easy, and early (striding)

      Turn, tilt, and tuck (front shoulder)

      Stride to balance

Figure 5.4 Proper head position: *(a)* both eyes on pitcher in setup; *(b)* head staying center throughout swing; *(c)* chin over rear shoulder at follow through.

Practice Tip

To work on proper head position, use the empty tee drill. After a batter strikes the ball off a batting tee, he keeps his head down and literally sees the empty tee. This drill teaches the batter to "nod to the ball," which reinforces proper head position both at contact and following contact.

Knob of the bat over the back foot at completion of the stride

One knee (only the front knee moves during the stride phase)

Front knee pinched (must remain closed on the landing of the stride foot)

b. **Block and drive:** The function of the front leg and front foot is to block the driving of the backside hip and knee. At the moment of impact the back heel is past the back toe, the back leg drives, and the front leg firms up, which causes the gap between the legs to narrow and forms the letter A with a closed front toe (figure 5.5). The energy and force are directed to the middle of the field.

Figure 5.5 Proper lower-half mechanics at impact: back heel past toe with the front foot blocked.

3. **Proper bat path:** The proper bat path is forward down to level, level, level. The knob of the bat goes from the back foot during launch to the front foot (figure 5.6*a*) during the attack phase of the swing and snaps back to the belly button at extension. The knob of the bat should never work up but always work down to level, level, level and be over the front foot at extension (figure 5.6*b*). The top hand stays on top of the bottom hand from start to finish. The shaft of the bat is close to the rear shoulder during the attack phase. John Cohen, head coach at Mississippi State University, coined the phrase "shaft to shoulder," which describes the handle of the bat grazing the apex of the back shoulder as it descends to the ball. A hitter must never allow the barrel to drop below the flight of the ball. Keeping the barrel above the hands (figure 5.6*c*) from start to finish allows the weight of the barrel and gravity to work in the hitter's favor. The hitter must "stop the drop"—keep the barrel above the hands through the entire swing—or the result will be a big-hop ground ball or a routine pop-up. The end of the bat should point toward the pitcher at extension (figure 5.6*d*).

The ultimate hitter has the correct head position from start to finish. He has good lower-half mechanics and executes proper stride mechanics,

Figure 5.6 Proper bat path: *(a)* knob of bat starts over back foot; *(b)* knob over front foot at extension; *(c)* barrel slightly above hands at impact; *(d)* end of bat pointing toward pitcher at extension.

allowing him to arrive at the launch position on time consistently and ready to strike the ball. He is then able to execute proper weight transfer from an explosive backside that is blocked by a stable front side and is able to maintain balance throughout. The proper bat path allows the hitter to hit line drives consistently. The flat stroke that produces line drives is the hallmark of a productive hitter. These three fundamentals must be mastered for the hitter to be consistent in his ability to function as part of a high-scoring offense.

When hitters start to break down their swing, they often focus on mechanics. Although faulty mechanics are certainly one possibility, more often than not it is something else. A hitter may experience difficulty swinging the bat for three reasons.

1. **Approach:** Having the right approach is the number one area to look at when determining why hitters are being unproductive. Without the proper plan or proper information a hitter will certainly fail. We have all seen "five o'clock hitters," those who perform well in batting practice but struggle in games. Hitters with functional mechanics usually struggle in games because of improper approach or poor timing. The good hitters watch the pitcher closely and understand his patterns. They anticipate certain pitches in certain situations. "The two most important fundamentals a hitter should know if he hopes to reach the majors and stay there are to learn as much as possible about the pitcher and be aware of the game situation when going to the plate," said Hall of Famer Frank Robinson. Remember, sit on what you are going to get, not what you want.

2. **Timing:** A hitter who has subpar mechanics but a great approach and good timing can do damage. Timing is more important than mechanics. The old saying that a pitcher's job is to get the hitter off-balance is still true today. A hitter must realize that waiting on the ball is a function of a good swing. Hall of Famer Tony Gwynn said, "Letting the ball travel deep in the zone is the toughest thing to do in hitting." A pitcher with a plus fastball is also challenging for the hitter because he has less time to react to the pitch. The bottom line is that a hitter must learn when to stride and learn to stride to balance to get his best swing off consistently.

3. **Mechanics:** Mechanical flaws need to be identified and corrected, but learning how to diagnose the flaw and where to start the correction process is an art. As with building a house the foundation is the most important part. When making adjustments to swing mechanics, start from the ground and work up. Put mechanics third on your list behind approach and timing.

Be careful to avoid assuming that all hitting problems are mechanical. They often are more the result of a bad approach or lack of a proper plan. Second, poor timing is an area that should be addressed. Sufficient time needs to be invested in drill work learning to adjust to various pitches. Finally, a hitter who is struggling needs to ask himself whether the problem is a bad approach, improper timing, or a mechanical flaw. He must not jump in the cage and start trying to fix mechanical flaws that might not be there. Productive hitters have the unique ability to zero in on exactly what the problem is before they try to correct it.

TWO THINGS THAT HITTERS CAN CONTROL

All hitters have control over two things: (1) when they swing and (2) when they stride.

When to Swing

All hitters must get good pitches to swing at to be productive. The hitter must be the puppeteer in terms of what he chooses to swing at. He cannot allow the pitcher to dictate which pitches he swings at. "When the pitcher is in a tough spot he will do his best to get you to go for bad balls," said legend Joe DiMaggio, adding, "But always remember, a walk is as good as a hit." Good hitters believe that the only thing the pitcher controls is where they drive the baseball in terms of the location of the pitch.

When to Stride

The second thing that a hitter controls is his stride. The purpose of the stride is to control timing. Pitchers obviously throw at different velocities, so hitters must be able to adjust accordingly. The hitter who is late on the fastball must start and complete his stride sooner because he cannot swing the bat until his front foot strikes the ground. If the hitter is early, he has the option of striding later, decreasing the amount of time that he must wait on the pitch and increasing his chances of arriving on time. A hitter must master the art of estimating the time of collision between bat and ball. The most difficult thing in hitting, according to Hall of Famer Tony Gwynn, is to let the ball travel deep into the strike zone before swinging. A hitter must learn to let the ball travel its proper distance before striking it. This task is extremely challenging, but the hitter can learn to adjust his timing with his stride.

For the hitter to be the puppeteer and not the puppet, he must control the controllables, which are what pitches he swings at and his timing. If the hitter does not control those two things, the roles become reversed and he becomes the puppet. The pitcher can manipulate him at his whim, and the hitter will lose the skirmish every time.

Practice Tip

Use visual cues to improve timing. For example, we tell hitters, "Ball up, heel up." When you break down the video of major-league hitters, you note that most start their load by lifting the front heel ("heel up") when the pitcher's throwing arm is parallel to the ground slightly after hand break ("ball up"). This method helps the hitter get in rhythm with the pitcher by getting his body in sync with the delivery and helping him arrive on time.

SQUARE TO CLOSE

A critical move that the hitter must make is going from his setup, or initial stance, to the launch position. Launch is defined as where the hitter is after the completion of the stride. As the name implies, the hitter launches the bat or swings the bat from this power base. A close look at major-league hitters at launch would reveal several key elements. The absolutes of a proper launch are as follows (figure 5.7):

1. The knees are inside the feet, and weight is on the balls of the feet.
2. The knob of the bat is over the back foot.
3. Have equal flexion and even distribution of weight.
4. The front side should be down and in.
5. The front foot lands closed with weight on the inside ball of the foot.
6. The front stride knee is pitched.
7. The barrel is over the head.
8. The front arm angle and bat angle are the same.
9. The lead arm angle has approximately 90 degrees of flexion.

The hitter strides to balance, landing in a closed position called launch. This move from setup to launch is extremely difficult for most hitters to master. The hitter must arrive in this position not only in a balanced manner but also on time and in rhythm to the pitch. The two biggest problems that hitters have when executing the stride are rushing and flying open.

Most hitters lack poise at the plate. A hitter's engine that is revving too high when he steps into the box will lead to a heavy stride, which lends itself to lunging and an improper launch. The old saying that a hitter's pump leads to a hitter's jump is true. The stride can be controlled by learning to stride "low, slow, and on the toe." The best advice that I ever received about how to control lunging from a mechanical perspective is to execute the

Figure 5.7 Proper launch: front side down and in with the front foot landing on the inside ball of the foot.

stride by moving only the front knee. Most hitters who lunge push off their rear leg on the stride, which causes both knees to move, resulting in improper balance at launch. The proper technique is to stride by reaching with the front foot and controlling the weight transfer during the stride phase by holding the weight over the inside of the back knee and not pushing the weight off the backside during the stride.

The second most common reason that hitters do not arrive at launch properly is that they land with their front side open. The proper technique is to land with the front side closed (figure 5.8a). Most high-school hitters go from a square stance, meaning that the chest is facing home plate, and land with the front foot and front shoulder open at the completion of the stride (figure 5.8b). Major-league hitters go from square in their setup to closed at the completion of their stride. They execute this by "turning, tilting, and tucking" the front shoulder at release and landing on the inside of the front foot with all 10 toes pointing toward home plate. The ability to go from square to closed is critical because it allows the hitter to adjust to various speeds and enhances plate coverage. Hitters who have difficulty performing this skill often "fire out of hand," meaning that they stride open when the pitcher is at release instead of striding closed at release.

Figure 5.8 *(a)* Proper landing with the front side closed and *(b)* incorrect landing with the front shoulder open.

Three simple drills can help players arrive at launch properly.

1. Mirror work: The player stands in front of a full-length mirror and performs stride mechanics. At the completion of his stride he should be in proper launch position, with the front side closed and the lead elbow pointing to the ground (figure 5.9a) and not higher than the back elbow (figure 5.9b).

2. Basketball drill: The player puts a basketball between his knees and performs a stride, keeping the basketball in place from the stride phase through the swing to launch. This drill emphasizes the importance of keeping the knees inside the feet (athletic position) from setup to launch. This drill is helpful for the player who opens his front knee, hip, or foot in the stride phase.

3. Tubing drills:

   a. Back side: Attach tubing to the knob of a bat and the opposite end to an immovable object behind the hitter. The hitter should feel tension in the tubing when in the setup position. At the completion of his stride the hitter should feel slack in the tubing as his hands load up, in, and back.

   b. Front side: Use the same setup except attach the tubing to an immovable object in front of the hitter. The tubing will now go from slack to tension when the hitter completes his stride and his hands load up, in, and back.

Figure 5.9 (a) Proper setup with the front elbow pointing at the ground and (b) incorrect technique with the front elbow higher than the back elbow.

BOTTOM HAND TRAVEL VERSUS HAND PIVOT

Hitters who have the ball jump off their bat have exceptional bat speed. They find the barrel of the bat on a consistent basis, and the barrel accelerates through contact. The top hand is evident on contact, and it stays above the bottom hand from start to finish. At no time does the hitter reverse his hands. If he allows his bottom hand to be above his top hand at contact, a slower swing results, leading to weakly hit balls. A batter starts with his top hand on top of his bottom hand in his initial stance, and he must maintain that relationship throughout the swing. The hitter must allow gravity and the weight of the barrel to work for him, not against him. The only way that gravity is the hitter's friend is to have the barrel stay above the hands throughout the swing. This can only be accomplished with a properly executed hand pivot in which the top hand passes the bottom hand between the hitter's feet.

Too many hitters push the baseball and do not hand pivot on the baseball. One of the functions of the bottom hand is to help direct the knob of the bat from the back foot in launch to the front foot in the attack phase and then back toward the belly button at contact and through extension (figure 5.10*a*). Many hitters tend to let the bottom hand travel past the midline of the body, which results in barrel lag and slower bat speed. When the bottom hand travels too far past the midline of the body before snapping back to the belly button, the knob has a tendency to travel upward, which promotes barrel drop and slows down the bat (figure 5.10*b*).

Figure 5.10 *(a)* Proper hand pivot with only the barrel being visible from behind at extension, indicating the knob has snapped back to the belly button and *(b)* an incorrect hand pivot with the bottom hand and knob pivots outside the body, indicating a swing flaw.

With the inception of the BBCOR bat, hitters will have to be more precise with their swing. Pushing the ball will not work with a wood bat or BBCOR bat. The hand pivot occurs between the feet, not outside the feet. The hands pivot inside the body if executed properly, and a coach standing behind the hitter would not see the knob of the bat (figure 5.11). If the hand pivot is executed incorrectly, the coach would see the hands pivot outside the bodyline. When the hitter is late with his hand pivot or his bottom hand travels too far, one of two problems occurs:

Figure 5.11   At extension the knob of the bat should point back to the belly button.

1. Under to the opposite field
2. Big-hop ground ball (strikes the 13-foot [4 m] dirt circle in front of home plate)

These two mis-hits will likely turn into outs because of their lag time, which increases the defense's ability to track down the ball and record the out. The three worst outs in baseball are

1. a routine fly ball,
2. a big-hop ground ball, and
3. a strikeout looking.

The first two are related to a poor hand pivot. Eliminating unproductive outs that do not create pressure is one of the goals of a high-scoring offense. Mastering the hand pivot minimizes these outs. Working on this small detail is worth the investment in helping hitters be productive.

A Common Misconception

Hitters may ask how they can hit a low pitch if the top hand is supposed to stay above the bottom hand. The answer is having the proper spine angle (figure 5.12). The front elbow should never be lifted (figure 5.13).

Figure 5.12 Proper bat path: batter executes the proper spine angle, as indicated by intersecting lines.

Figure 5.13 Improper bat path: lifting the front elbow will cause the barrel to drop below the hands.

DRILLS

Performing drills correctly is one small piece of building the ultimate hitter. Knowing what hitting drills to perform, which drills are appropriate for each hitter, how to evaluate performance in each drill, and how to progress lead-up drills to shape the ultimate hitter is critical. To be productive for an individual hitter, a drill should be challenging and exploit a weakness. For the progressive drills listed here, the important point is how they are performed, evaluated, and measured so that the hitter can get critical feedback and continue to improve over time.

Tee Work

1. Use a high tee or low tee, never right down the middle.
2. Always use the full length of the tunnel to allow tracking the flight of the ball or hit long on the field.
3. In your initial setup, line up the tee even with your front foot (figure 5.14a) to hit the ball straight back. When you get in the box look down at the end of the tunnel and have open focus to simulate seeing the whole pitcher.

Figure 5.14 *(a)* Measure up to ensure proper plate coverage and contact point, end of bat on outside corner, knob of bat on front toe; *(b)* strike the inside of the two seams; *(c)* backspin the ball to the backside of the tunnel.

4. When setting the ball on the tee, align the two seams vertically and attack the inside seam of the baseball closest to you as a hitter (figure 5.14*b*).

5. At the completion of the stride, as you start your swing turn your head to the baseball (figure 5.14*c*). Your goal is to carry the baseball the full length of the tunnel with backspin. Hit the ball off the sweet spot of the bat consistently. Avoid hitting big-hop ground balls (balls that are hit down within 13 feet [4 m] of the plate) or pop-ups (balls that hit the top net of the tunnel).

6. Hitting balls off the tee into a net a few feet away is not advised because you cannot receive proper feedback on the flight of the ball.

Side Flips

Setup

Use the full length of the batting tunnel.

Equipment

1. Bat
2. Baseballs
3. Throw-down home plate

Execution

The hitter should stand on a quarter-inch (60 mm) piece of wood that elevates his heels (to ensure proper body posture and energy flow in a straight line) when hitting a ball thrown from the side.

The person with the baseball should show the ball to the hitter, be on one knee (figure 5.15a), and then have his hand go straight down about 2 feet (60 cm) and straight back up (to enhance the feel of load) when throwing the ball to the hitter from the side (figure 5.15b). The ball should be tossed so that it lands on the plate and does not travel into the hitter.

Variations

The person tossing the baseball has the liberty of moving the ball to all quadrants of the strike zone and repeating zones that the hitter has trouble with.

Coaching points

The hitter should not be rushed between repetitions. He should maintain balance from start to finish.

Common error and correction

The person feeding the ball often throws the ball too close (into) the hitter. Focus on flipping the ball over the plate.

Figure 5.15 Side flips: *(a)* show the ball to the hitter then let the hand go straight down and straight back up to flip the baseball; *(b)* flip the baseball to the front edge of the plate.

Underhand Front Toss

Setup

Use the full length of the batting tunnel. This drill is performed straight on to the hitter approximately 20 feet (6.1 m) away.

Equipment

1. Bat
2. Baseballs
3. L-frame of flip screen
4. Portable strike zone catch net

Execution

Some people like to do underhand toss seated, but the preferred method is a two step walk-up. This approach is advised to allow the batter to get in rhythm with the pitcher (figure 5.16a). The benefit of underhand toss is that the pitcher can locate pitches better and perform more repetitions while the hitter improves his stroke on a wide variety of pitch locations (figure 5.16b).

Variations

Many variations of this underhand front toss drill can be used. For example, the flips can be extremely firm to simulate velocity or extremely soft to simulate slow pitches. A breaking ball can be simulated by bouncing the ball, and a combination of these is the most realistic. The pitcher can also throw hard in and soft away and repeat each quadrant when the hitter fails to put a good swing on that particular pitch. After the hitter has hit the ball hard, the pitcher rotates the quadrant.

Adding a radar gun to this drill makes it more viable in terms of feedback and determining exit speed and adds fun to the typical front toss for the hitter. The person holding the radar gun stands behind the back net and gets the exit speed of the ball coming off the bat from a front toss. A stalker radar gun is preferred because it picks up both the pitch and the ball coming off the bat. If the underhand toss is under 25 miles per hour (40 km/h), the Jugs gun will not pick it up and will show only the exit speed of the ball coming off the bat. Productive hitters hit the ball hard, consistently, straight back in drill work. A way to measure that success is exit speed and the place where the batter hits the ball. College hitters should be in the exit speed range of 87 to 90 miles per hour (140 to 145 km/h); anything about 90 usually indicates power.

Coaching points

1. The full length of the tunnel is preferred because the hitter can track and follow the flight of the ball. The goal is to carry the ball all the way to the back of the net without hitting either side, the top, or the bottom first.

2. Placing an 8-foot (2.4 m) square target at the back of the net with numbers is a way to make the drill competitive, encourage hitters to hit the ball straight back, and provide them feedback. Hitters like to compete against one another and can play a point game when they use the hitting target.

Common error and correction

The biggest error is that hitters fail to load at the proper time. The hitter should load when the pitcher's arm is back.

Figure 5.16 Underhand front toss: *(a)* pitcher using a two-step walk-up approach so the hitter can time his load; *(b)* coach using radar gun to check exit speed.

Batting Practice

Using a proper progression in batting practice is critical in reinforcing the proper approach, timing, and swing. Incorporating bat-control skills, bunting, and various counts serves to reinforce the concept of a complete hitter. Here is an example of a batting practice plan:

Round 1:

Graduate

Four swings, one bunt

Fastballs, less than two strikes

The hitter tries to hit four power ground balls to the back side of the field that make contact with the grass first and not the 13-foot (4 m) dirt circle in front of home plate. Early in the season we tell our players they must graduate from this round by hitting three ground balls out of four off the grass before they can move on to the next round. A ball that makes contact in the dirt in front of home plate is considered a swing flaw, a big-hop ground ball that would increase the range of the infielder. We start this way so that the hitter can let the ball travel deep into the zone, learn to keep the club head above the flight of the ball, and work through the baseball to produce backspin on the ball off the grass to the back side of the field. Executing this skill reinforces the bat-control skills needed to move runners and hit with two strikes. After those four swings, the hitter executes a drag bunt and runs out of the box to a short base 30 feet (9.1 m) down the line.

Round 2:

Bat control

Four swings, one bunt

Fastballs, less than two strikes

The drill starts with two hit-and-runs. The batter must swing at the pitch and hit the ball on the ground outside the middle of the infield to prevent an easy double play. Next are two hit-and-run drives, which the batter tries to drive into the gaps. A hit-and-run drive is typically executed when the pitcher falls behind in the count 2-0 or 3-1. The offense predicts that the pitcher will throw a fastball, turns the hitter loose, and starts the runner at first. The batter will likely get a fastball and drive the ball into the gap, and the base runner who is stealing will score from first base. With a 3-1 count the hitter swings only at a strike and takes the pitch if it is a ball, but either way the play works. The round ends with the batter pushing a bunt up the first-base line and running full speed through the short base.

Round 3:

Positive count

Four swings, one slash

Fastballs, less than two strikes

The batter takes four swings on fastballs. This round simulates a cripple count (2-0, 3-1, 3-0), which are hitters' counts. We want hitters looking for a fastball and driving the baseball with backspin. At the completion of those four swings, the hitter executes a slash. A right-handed hitter shows bunt, pulls the bat back, and pulls the ball from the six hole to the third-base line. A left-handed hitter hits the ball on the ground out of the middle.

Round 4:

RBIs

Four swings, one bunt

Mix fastballs and curveballs, less than two strikes

The round starts with a runner at second base and no outs (over and in). The hitter drives the ball hard on the ground to the right side of the infield to advance the runner. The second pitch starts with a runner at second base and two outs (two-out RBI). The goal for the hitter is to hit a line drive down to the middle of the field. A good way for the hitter to get feedback is it to hit the L-frame in batting practice. We do not want to hit a fly ball with two outs to end the inning because it creates no pressure. Hitting the L-frame reinforces hitting a line drive down with two outs and a man in scoring position. The third swing is with a runner at third and the infield back. The goal is to hit a hard ground ball through the middle and stay away from third base. The fourth swing is with runner at third and the infield in. The goal is to attack the inside part of the baseball and drive the ball into the outfield on a ball that is up in the strike zone. The fifth pitch is a safety squeeze, using a bunt to produce an RBI to end the round.

Round 5:

Two Strikes

Four swings

Mix pitches, all with two strikes

This round uses four swings with two strikes. The batter makes his two-strike adjustments. He chokes up, moves up in the box, widens his base, and gets closer to the plate. His approach is "late and on top." The batting practice pitcher mixes the pitches and simulates a 1-2 count in which the hitter does not know what's coming so that he can practice his two-strike approach. The

(continued) ➡

Batting Practice   *(continued)*

fifth swing simulates a 3-2 count, and the runner at first base is running. The hitter's job is to hit the ball hard on the ground if the pitch is a strike and take the pitch if it is a ball.

Round 6:

Specialty

Four swings

Fast or slow, vary location

If time permits, a specialty round can be added to help prepare the hitter for the type of pitcher that he will face that day. The BP pitcher throws pitches that simulate the starting pitcher's repertoire. For example, he could throw a plus fastball, curveballs below the zone, pitches from a soft lefty, or pitches from a pitcher who tries to dominate the outer half.

CHAPTER 6

Creating Pressure With the Bunt

If our teams can bunt, we have the weaponry to attack and score even on excellent defensive teams or in adverse weather conditions, with wind blowing in or when it's cold and wet.

Gordie Gillespie, head baseball coach, University of St. Francis

The bunting game should be the foundation of your offensive arsenal. Augie Garrido, legendary head coach of the University of Texas Longhorns, in a 2002 article in *Collegiate Baseball* stated the value of a solid bunting game:

> *As far as total offense goes, the bunting game does play a role in that. There are three phases to offense. You must get on base. You must advance runners into scoring position. And then you must score runners. The bunting game allows a batter to do all three. You can bunt for a base hit to get on base. You can bunt to advance runners, obviously. You can squeeze bunt or safety squeeze to score runners.* (Lou Pavovich, Jr., "Small ball: A Secret Weapon," p.6, 2002)

A high-powered offense has a reputation for being able to execute the bunting game at any time and at any spot in the batting order. This ability gives the offense an advantage because the defense must be on its toes on every pitch. "Bunting is one of the first lessons our new players learn," said George Horton, former head coach at Cal State Fullerton ("Small ball," 2002).

Defensive miscues are often a result of three things in terms of reacting to the short game: good placement, deception (the hitter's ability to disguise the fact that he is bunting), and the bunter's ability to get down the line quickly. The correct execution of the bunting game creates confusion on the part of the defense because they do not know when or where the offense might use all their various bunting weapons. The proper mentality for the bunting game is that there is no such thing as a sacrifice bunt. The high-scoring offense has a mentality that they are not giving up an out but are simply moving a runner up 90 feet (27.4 m). The best thing that could happen is for the defense to hurry and create a two-base error.

Well-placed bunts create pressure by making the defense hurry their throws and forcing the corner infielders to shallow up to counter the threat of the bunt. The bunt game dictates defensive positioning, which gives the hitter a better chance of getting a base hit. The infielder has decreased his normal range by coming in toward the hitter. For every step that a defender takes in toward the hitter, he loses two steps, one to his left and one to his right. So the threat of the bunt helps the hitter in multiple ways. If a hitter can get the third baseman, for example, to move in three steps, the fielder is losing nine steps in his range and ability to defend the hitter. The batter's goal is not just to advance the runner or get a base hit but to place the bunt in a "kill zone," forcing the defender to pick up the ball under duress and possibly throw the ball away, resulting in multiple runners gaining 180 feet (54.9 m), not just 90 feet (27.4 m).

The bunting game also affects where the defense has to play. For example, when an offensive player is known as both a good drag bunter and a good push bunter, both corner infielders must come in to defend against these bunts. As a result, both lose lateral range, which increases the chance of driving the ball past them. The best thing about creating pressure with the bunting game is that everyone in the lineup can contribute to the offense. "Bunting is a way of giving an offensive player an easier way to contribute to the offensive rally," said Garrido. "That's my first concern—finding ways to help the player be successful. Bunting is a heck of a lot easier than hitting" ("Small ball," 2002).

Without the threat of the short game, the pitcher can lock into cruise control and focus simply on trying to retire the batter. He doesn't have to worry about defending his position. The offense wants the pitcher to feel uncomfortable and to be distracted and nervous about fielding his position. High-powered offenses have offensive spontaneity. In other words, they have the ability to take advantage of what the defense gives them, but just as important they have the skill set to make it happen. For example, if the corner infielders are playing back, the offense can exploit that positioning by using the bunt. The opposite is also true: If the defense is playing the corners in to take away the bunt, the hitter has gained an advantage because the corner infielders have lost lateral range. Hitters should always look for opportunities to drag or push bunt, but only when the defense is out of position.

Another important plus for the bunting game is that it forces the defense to communicate. Failure to communicate or miscommunication can lead to errors. Well-placed bunts create pressure because they force the defense to execute in a timely manner, require the defenders to communicate, and test their ability to focus.

THE MORE IMPORTANT THE GAME, THE MORE IMPORTANT THE BUNT

Bunting in big games is paramount because defenses have trouble executing under pressure when something of magnitude is on the line. Before the game starts, the team that is proficient at the short game has an advantage over the team that is not. Advancing runners, scoring runners, and even getting on base by the bunt are valuable tools when facing the good pitching possessed by most tournament teams that are in a position to win a championship. Many playoff games have been won by players bunting into a tense infield defense.

Two fundamental skills at which offenses need to be proficient in championship games are executing bunts and hitting the curveball. From the first practice of the year, work on the bunting game and hitting the curveball because late in the season, when the game is on the line, batters will have to get a bunt down or hit the breaking ball to win the game. Productive offensive teams are proficient at executing the bunt and are able to hit the breaking ball with men in scoring position. All the training that a team does in terms of the short game is to prepare them to win in the postseason. To win in the BBCOR era, you must be proficient at small ball.

TYPES OF BUNTS

Typically, in the latter third of the game, one run becomes more critical than it is early in the game. Any time that a team is playing for one run, well-placed bunts are extremely valuable. A high-production offense must perfect the bunting game so that they can push that last run across in a tight ballgame. Our goal for this skill is three well-placed bunts per game. The primary bunts are the following:

1. Sacrifice or kill-zone bunt on either the first-base side or the third-base side.
2. Drag bunt down the third-base line.
3. Push bunt by the pitcher at the second baseman.
4. Safety squeeze toward the first baseman.
5. Squeeze bunt away from the pitcher.
6. Slash bunt in conjunction with the sacrifice bunt.

Any combination of these bunts would be included in the tabulation of three well-placed bunts per game. A high-scoring offense is multifaceted, and bunting is a skill that a team must have in its repertoire to be flexible and help it score runs when it is not hitting.

Sacrifice Bunt

The sacrifice bunt is a weapon that even high-powered offenses need to use to score runs. The sacrifice bunt is primarily used late in the game, in the eighth or ninth inning, to help manufacture one run. The sacrifice bunt, as the name suggests, has the bunter give himself up to advance the base runner. At times the offense does not need to play for the big inning but instead plays for one run because that is all they need to win the ballgame. At that time the sacrifice bunt is a viable option.

In a true sacrifice situation, timing is a critical factor in consistent execution, and an early setup is imperative. The batter should move up in the box, stand on top of the plate, and square around early using an upper-body pivot just as the pitcher is coming set. The front foot should be slightly closed and flat, while the back foot is up on the toe. The bat is held at eye level at the top of the strike zone, and the back elbow is bent down into the body (figure 6.1). The bunter must sight the ball over the top of the bat and maintain this posture throughout the process. The bottom hand is on top of the bat 4 to 5 inches (10 to 12 cm) up from the knob. The top hand is loose with a pistol grip and placed at the label. The bunter should focus on the top of the ball and make contact there. The back knee lowers the club head to the low strike.

The early turn gives the bunt away, but the tradeoff is that the batter has plenty of time to get set with an exaggerated knee flex (figure 6.2a), the barrel at the top of the strike zone, the hands extended, and the eyes behind the blade (figure 6.2b). The early turn also allows the batter to pull the bat back to slash in the event that the defense overplays the bunt. Placement and pace are the keys to the sacrifice bunt. The bunter must preset his angle and be extremely steady, making sure that he does not jab at the baseball. Instead, he catches the baseball off the end of the bat. To

Figure 6.1 Sacrifice bunt: bunter up in the box and on top of the plate.

reach the low strike, the bunter must lower his knees and his chest but not drop the barrel, because doing so will often result in a pop-up.

The sacrifice should be the first bunting skill mastered. After that, the logical progression would be mastery of the drag bunt, followed by the push bunt, safety squeeze, and squeeze bunt, in succession. The order is a reflection of the frequency of each bunt during games.

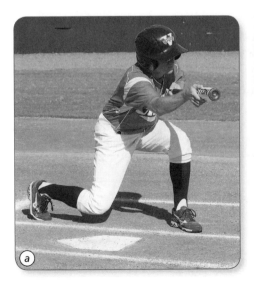

Figure 6.2 Sacrifice bunt: *(a)* exaggerated knee flex and *(b)* hands extended with eyes behind the blade.

The time for the sacrifice bunt in the high-powered offense is late in the ballgame. Research indicates the following, as noted in *The Book on the Book*:

> *The break-even point for a sacrifice is 80%; that is, it has to work about 80% of the time to have any utility. Amazingly, as with many statistics in the highly symmetrical game that is baseball, 80% is almost precisely the figure at which the sacrifice does work in the major leagues. In 2003, the major-league success rate for the sacrifice was about 79%. (Felber, 2005)*

The sacrifice bunt must be practiced repeatedly to ensure that your team's success rate falls into that 80% range that makes it worth the tradeoff. Failure to execute the sacrifice bunt has cost many teams a victory. Great bunting teams can sacrifice bunt, and they do this by squaring around early, bunting the ball with proper pace away from the pitcher, never jabbing at the ball, and not running out of the box early. Players need to remember to bunt first and then run.

Kill Zone Versus Sacrifice

The kill zone is an area located adjacent to the foul lines 25 to 35 feet (7.6 to 10.6 m) from home plate and approximately 10 feet (3 m) wide (figure 6.3). A skilled bunter can place a drag bunt or a sacrifice bunt in this kill zone. A bunt in this area creates pressure because it is placed away from the catcher, pitcher, and corner infielder, and, in most cases, it forces the fielder to hurry when he is trying to retire the batter. The goal of the bunter is to place a bunt in the kill zone every time. This mentality of putting the ball in a good spot and creating pressure is the proper mind-set of a high-scoring offensive player. His priorities are to place bunts in kill zones, create pressure, advance the lead runner, and, lastly, to reach base safely.

As the name suggests, the sacrifice bunt surrenders an out in exchange for advancing the runner. It is most often used to score a single run late in the game. The kill zone bunt, on the other hand, has pressure as its primary objective, which the offense hopes will result in a multiple-run inning. The kill zone bunt will not only advance the lead runner 90 feet (27.4 m) but also afford the offense the opportunity to have a big inning by not giving up one of its 27 precious outs. Learning to deaden the ball so that it rolls only in the 25- to 35-foot (7.6 to 10.6 m) box is an art that requires many hours of practice.

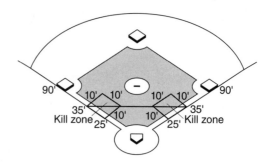

Figure 6.3 Kill zones.

The number one skill needed to deaden the ball properly is making contact with the ball off the end of the bat. This skill requires having soft hands and catching the ball rather than pushing at it. The second most important skill is applying the proper bat angle to use the foul lines. Proper bat angle means not only using the correct directional alignment but also keeping the barrel of the bat above the knob at all times. Third is proper timing, which means not showing the bunt until the pitcher is at his release point.

With sufficient practice, this bunt can be mastered. It is a powerful weapon in creating run-scoring opportunities. According to Augie Garrido,

> *If you do not practice bunting, your players will probably not be able to do it during a game. If you do not practice it in gamelike situations where you have high intensity, you will probably not be able to bunt during games. The best way to do this is for the players to play games, with high intensity concerning the bunting game. Have them hit targets on the field with their bunts. You can also have two-man teams going against each other, two-man teams for competition. ("Small ball," 2002)*

Drag Bunt

The drag bunt is the easiest bunt for most players to master. The drag bunt is placed down the third-base line within the 25- to 35-foot (7.6 to 10.6 m) kill box and 10 feet (3 m) from the third-base line (figure 6.4). Learning to show late—meaning after release—and creating momentum are two important skills that proficient drag bunters must master. Players have to remember to bunt first and then run. Good placement is paramount. The goal is to bunt the ball on the chalk or have it roll foul, never back to the mound.

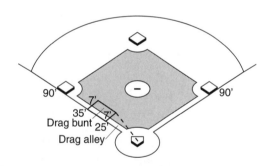

Figure 6.4   Drag bunt zone.

Right-Handed Batter Technique

1. **Grip:** The bunter slides the right hand up the barrel so that there is only about 6 inches (15 cm) between the top hand and the end of the bat (figure 6.5*a*). The top hand grip should be like a trigger finger on a weapon. The bottom hand is approximately 4-6 inches from the bottom. Both hands have a relaxed grip, which promotes deadening the ball.

2. **Bat angle:** The barrel is out in front of home plate. Both hands are in front of the front hip, and the barrel should be parallel to the first-base line to create the proper angle. The barrel of the bat remains higher than the knob at all times. The bunter keeps the front elbow tight against the front side, about chest high, and the back elbow down.

3. **Stance:** The bunter should transfer his weight by dropping his back foot back slightly. He transfers all his weight onto his front foot, which increases plate coverage, facilitates momentum toward first base, and brings his eyes level with the ball. A pitch on the outer half is easier to lean on and helps the bunter get out of the box quickly. Most drag bunters like to stand farther off the plate. The bunter stands tall and works down to the ball. He also starts off the plate and works into the plate.

4. **Head position:** The bunter's head should be even with the flight of the ball coming in and as close to the barrel as possible.

5. **Getting out of the box:** Placement and the stopwatch are directly linked. The bunter leads with his back foot (figure 6.5*b*),

Figure 6.5 Right-handed drag bunt: *(a)* end of the bat extends with both hands in front of lead hip; *(b)* bunter leads with back foot; *(c)* exits the box in a straight line.

makes certain that he is running in a straight line as he begins to release the bat (figure 6.5c), and touches the front of the bag with an inward body lean. Every 10th of a second matters!

Left-Handed Batter Technique

1. **Grip:** The bunter slides the left hand up the barrel so that there is only about 6 inches (15 cm) between the top hand and the end of the bat (figure 6.6a). The top hand grip should be like a trigger finger on a weapon. The bottom hand is slid up from the bottom 6 inches. Both hands have a relaxed grip, which promotes deadening the ball.

2. **Bat angle:** The left arm is extended in front of the bunter's body and in front of home plate. The bat is parallel to the first-base line, and the barrel is elevated above the knob.

3. **Stance:** To disguise the drag bunt, the left-handed drag bunter takes a short stride as if he is going to hit and then takes a short jab step with his rear leg toward home plate (figure 6.6b). This movement gets the bat into fair territory and keeps the bunter from pulling out before bunting the ball. Getting the left foot down before the ball leaves the pitcher's hand is advantageous. Most of the bunter's weight should be on his rear leg. He must lower his center of gravity by dropping his hips.

4. **Head position:** The bunter's head should be even with the flight of the ball coming in and as close to the barrel as possible.

5. **Getting out of the box:** After bunting the ball, the left-handed bunter lead steps to first with his left foot (figure 6.6c). He must not transfer the weight early to his right leg but must hold the weight on his left leg while bunting the ball. If he leaves the bunt early by transferring his weight to his right foot, correct ball placement will be difficult.

Figure 6.6 Left-handed drag bunt: *(a)* batter takes short jab step toward home plate with his left foot; *(b)* bat is extended in front of home plate; *(c)* bunter exits the box in a straight line to first base.

The most important technique required to produce a good bunt is for the bunter to get his face behind the blade, or barrel, of the bat. The bunter must feel as if he is sighting a gun. His face is extremely close to the barrel, and he understands that the barrel and the face are attached to one another, where the barrel goes the face must also go. Another important technique for the drag bunter is to make sure that the top hand is fully extended before and during the bunting of the ball. This positioning will eliminate jabbing or pushing at the ball, which is one of the most common mistakes that bunters make. The rule of thumb is that the looser and closer the grip is to the end of the bat, the softer the bunt will be.

Push Bunt

The push bunt is possibly the most underutilized bunt in baseball. The push bunt is difficult to master, but it is an effective weapon because most teams do not practice defending it. The push bunt is the only bunt that requires the person bunting the ball to do so off the barrel of the bat. The objective is to have the ball roll past the pitcher, forcing the second baseman or the first baseman to charge in to field it. The push bunt is a good choice against a left-handed pitcher who falls toward the third-base line after release.

Key elements of the push bunt are the following:

1. The ball must be bunted off the barrel.
2. The target of the bunt is the Bermuda triangle, the area between the pitcher and the first baseman and in front of the second baseman.
3. The ball should first strike the ground in the grass, not the dirt. Skimming the ball off the grass first ensures that it has proper pace to get by the pitcher.

Right-Handed Batter Technique

1. As the pitcher starts his arm up, the bunter takes a drop step toward the back outside corner of the batter's box with his right foot. At release, the batter steps toward the second baseman, also with the right foot.
2. The bunter steps toward the second baseman and brings the bat into bunting position. He extends both arms with a strong inverted right-handed grip and directs the barrel at the second baseman to bunt the ball with good pace at the second baseman (figure 6.7a).
3. The bunter must make sure that he drops his center of gravity and gets his chest even with the flight of the ball (figure 6.7b). He should stand closer to the plate because pushing the ball is easier when he doesn't have to reach for the pitch.
4. The barrel must stay above the hands, even on a low pitch (figure 6.7c).

Figure 6.7 Right-handed push bunt: *(a)* bunter takes a drop toward the back corner with his right foot; *(b)* the bunter steps toward the second baseman and brings the bat into bunting position; *(c)* the barrel must stay above the hands for successful execution.

Left-Handed Batter Technique

1. Just before the pitcher releases the ball, the batter steps toward the second baseman with his rear foot. As he steps, he brings the bat forward to shoulder height or slightly below with a straight left arm (figure 6.8*a*).

2. He makes sure that the top hand is fully extended. The palm of the left hand is facing the second baseman, and the bat is held firmly. He bunts the ball off the barrel in the direction of the Bermuda triangle (figure 6.8*b*).

3. The bunter maintains an athletic posture and makes sure that he never rises (stands up) during the bunt to ensure that his eyes remain on the same plane throughout execution. He moves aggressively toward first with his right foot as he releases the bat (figure 6.8*c*).

Figure 6.8 Left-handed push bunt: *(a)* left arm extended with a strong inverted left-handed grip; *(b)* proper bat angle directed at the "Bermuda triangle"; *(c)* exiting the box with momentum toward the second baseman.

If a mistake is made in executing the push bunt, it should be too firm and away from the pitcher toward first base. The push bunt is an exceptional weapon against a left-handed pitcher whose follow-through takes him toward the third-base line, which enlarges the push bunt lane.

Squeeze and Safety Squeeze

The suicide squeeze is an all-or-nothing proposition for the bunter. The bunter must bunt the ball regardless of whether the pitch is a ball or strike. His only real objective is to get the ball down and away from pitcher. The runner on third does not start to run until the pitcher's front foot is down or the pitcher is at release. Like the runner breaking for home, the bunter performs his task late, meaning that he does not show until release or foot strike, thus disguising his intention as long as possible. If the bunter gets the bunt down in fair territory, the run will most likely score.

The squeeze bunt is a late-turn sacrifice bunt. Most teams use an acknowledgement sign to ensure that everyone is on the same page. After the bunter has received the squeeze sign, he must give an acknowledgement sign so that both the base runner and the coach know that the play is on. In addition, the base runner must acknowledge that he has received the sign.

The safety squeeze differs from the suicide squeeze in that the bunter has the freedom to bunt only strikes. The safety squeeze, as its name implies, provides the offense with a certain degree of safety because it is not an all-out proposition. The bunter bunts strikes, and the runner breaks when he sees down-angle contact made. The technique requires the right-handed batter to show at release and walk his back foot forward, which helps keep the barrel up. His objective is to bunt the ball toward first base away from the pitcher. The base runner breaks when he sees down-angle contact and runs regardless of direction, but he will be able to get back if he sees the bunt popped up. The best time to run the safety squeeze is when runners are at first and third base because the first baseman has to hold the runner, which delays his ability to charge the bunt. The advantage of the first-and-third safety squeeze is that you score the run from third and advance the runner from first.

Slash

The slash is used in conjunction with the sacrifice bunt. If the defense, especially the third baseman, charges overaggressively, the bunter should recoil from the bunting position and hit the ball on the ground away from the second-base bag. The batter squares around early using an upper-body bunting technique when the pitcher comes set. When he sees the third baseman charge, the bunter recoils from the bunting position and pulls a ground ball into the six hole or toward the charging third baseman. A left-handed hitter can hit the ball anywhere on the ground, but he must keep it away from the second-base bag. The hitter should only hit a pitch that he can direct at the defense's weakness.

Also called the butcher boy play, the slash is a useful weapon against defenses that overplay on a sacrifice bunt. One of the big mistakes in executing the slash is pulling the bat back late and not being ready to swing the bat. The proper timing is to show bunt early when the pitcher comes set and to pull the bat back when the pitcher breaks his hands (figure 6.9a). That way the hitter is set and can get on top of a fastball. Additionally, when the bunter squares around he is choked up with his left hand and his right hand, but when he recoils to swing he takes his right hand to his left hand, creating an exaggerated choke grip (figure 6.9b) and gaining more bat control.

Figure 6.9 Slash: *(a)* batter squares around to bunt when pitcher comes set; *(b)* batter pulls bat back for slash when the pitcher breaks his hands.

COMMON PROBLEMS

Coaches and players need to be aware of several common problems in the short game:

1. **Not getting the face close enough to the blade, or barrel, of the bat.** A good coaching point is to tell the bunter to get his face close to the barrel as if he is aiming a rifle at a target. "A good bunter is fearless and must take his nose to the baseball to be successful," says Tom Robson, former major-league hitting coach (Robson, 2003).

2. **Running out of the box too soon.** Bunters have a tendency to want to get out of box in a hurry, which compromises placement. A bunt placed in a good spot creates pressure because it forces the defender to run a long distance, break down his steps, and make an accurate throw on the run. Bunters need to remember to bunt before they run.

3. **Top hand not far enough up on the barrel.** The goal in bunting is to deaden the ball, but to do that the hitter must bunt the ball off the end of the bat. By placing the top hand 6 inches (15 cm) from the end of the bat and bunting the ball between the end of the bat and his hand, the player can bunt the ball in the small 6-inch space at the end of the bat.

4. **Not getting the top hand extended and presetting the proper angle.** "The top hand always creates the angle of the bat for placement," according to Robson (2003). Inexperienced bunters jab at the ball and bunt too many balls back toward the pitcher. The bunter should get his top hand extended, which creates a better angle away from the pitcher and makes it virtually impossible for the bunter to jab at the baseball because his top hand is already fully locked, which prevents the top arm from extending toward the bunt.

5. **Not getting low enough.** Bunters often stand too high and assume an unathletic posture. A teaching point would be for the bunter to get his face even with the flight of the ball coming in so that he can more easily see the ball and get it down. "Good bunters have quiet heads and hands," says Robson (2003).

6. **Improper plate coverage.** Many bunters do not move up in the box and do not get close enough to the plate. They end up reaching for balls that they should be able to handle, which creates barrel drop and bad placement. Coaches can stand behind a protective net in practice when the players are bunting to make sure that when they square around the bat covers the entire width of the plate and is in front of the plate. The bat head should be in fair territory.

DRILLS

The following drills are among my favorites because they provide good variety in your practice plan. Sometimes you have to exaggerate a movement in the training process for the players to gain the kinesthetic feel of correct body placement. The following drills focus on overteaching steadiness, to prevent jabbing at the ball, and getting as low as possible so that the player feels his head in the middle of his body, assumes the correct athletic posture, and does not run out of the box early. The use of a live arm helps with timing and a pitching machine allows players to get used to velocity. Finally, the use of a paddle glove can be extremely useful in an indoor setting.

Statue Bunting

Have the player bunt the ball and not move at all. We want the bat not to move at all after the bunter has set the proper angle and the ball has exited the bat. We also want the player's face as close to the barrel as possible. We are simulating firing a rifle at a target. Players should be sure and steady.

One-Knee Bunting

Have players bunt off the back knee early in the season (figure 6.10). This drill helps them get low, stabilizes the head by placing it in the middle of the body, and makes it impossible to run out of the box. As the off-season progresses have them just tap the back knee and come up several inches from the ground. This action creates an exaggerated knee flex when executing a sacrifice bunt.

Figure 6.10   One-knee bunting.

Four-Base Bunting

Setup

The setup for this drill is to have four offensive players at each base. One player is the bunter, one player is the catcher, one player is the pitcher, and the fourth player is the fielder. Use bunting corner (see figure 6.3 earlier in the chapter) that has been marked off by paint or tape with 10-foot-wide (3 m) kill zones 25 to 35 feet (7.6 to 10.6 m) down the first- and third-base lines. Throw-down bases are positioned halfway between each base at approximately 45 feet (13.7 m).

Equipment

1. Pitching machine (or live arm)
2. Throw down plate or base
3. Paint or tape for markings

Execution

The pitcher goes from the stretch. All bunters perform the same bunt four times as they move up to the next base. The objective is to perform each bunt and run full speed through the short base. Perform bunts in bunting corner down the third- and first-base lines. The markings help players get immediate visual feedback about whether they are bunting the ball with proper pace and direction. Players execute proper baserunning form by running in a straight line, touching the front of the base with an upper-body lean, and breaking down after they pass the base, looking right for an overthrow and left for an opening (discussed in more detail in chapter 7). If, for example, you are working on a drag bunt, the bunter could start at home plate and execute a drag bunt four times as he goes around the bases. When the player returns to home plate a new player executes the same sequence. After every player has performed a drag bunt the rotation starts again with a different bunt. The great thing about this drill is that players bunt off a live arm and run the bases full speed.

Variations

On some days ask the bunters to bunt breaking balls. In games pitchers will invariably throw breaking balls because hitters do not practice bunting against curveballs. They usually end up fouling them off and finding themselves in a two-strike count. Bunting off the pitching machine has value because the bunter has to execute off velocity. Learning to bunt off velocity helps players overcome the fear of squaring around and putting the face close to the barrel in a controlled environment. Fear is real, and getting on top of the plate with your face close the blade does require some toughness.

Coaching points

The best thing to do when bunting off a machine is to use leather baseballs that have Kevlar seams because they feed better and the player gets a more real sensation off the bat, as opposed to dimple balls that are made of rubber and have a trampoline effect when they come off the bat.

Figure 6.11 Taping the end of the bat is a valuable technique to teach deadening a bunt.

Another teaching aid is to tape the last 6 inches (15 cm) of the bat as a reminder to the bunter to bunt the ball off the end of the bat (figure 6.11). This technique deadens the ball and makes it possible to kill the ball in the optimal 25- to 35-foot hurry zones.

Common errors and corrections

The most common errors are improper bat angle and bunting the ball too firmly. Make sure bunters preset their angles on sac bunts and bunt the ball off the end of the bat.

Paddle Glove

The bunter places a paddle glove on his top hand and performs bunts off a pitching machine (figure 6.12). The objective is to teach players the importance of catching the ball with the top hand. To reinforce that, all bunting is dictated by an extended or locked top hand. The face is as close to the glove as possible, just like when playing catch. This drill adds variety to the everyday practice plan.

Figure 6.12 Paddle glove: reinforce the importance of the top hand in directing bunts.

One of the benefits of a team drill is that players get a better sense of the speed of the game. Small game is a great way to challenge batters to execute well-placed bunts and defenders to execute under pressure. In addition, both the defense and the offense develop a heightened awareness of the impact of well-placed bunts. Obviously, bunts that are in a kill zone force the defense to hurry, while bunts that are poorly placed are easy to defend. Plus, players enjoy competing against one another.

Small Game

Setup

The main field (infield) should be used. This drill is composed of all bunts performed against a complete infield defense versus a live arm or a pitching machine. A runner starts at first base with no outs. A hitter is at the plate, and a third-base coach gives the signals.

Equipment

1. Pitching machine (or live arm)
2. Throw-down base
3. Cones

Execution

The objective is to bunt the lead runner or runners around the bases using all the various bunts. The defense plays it live and communicates. Players are required to back up the appropriate bases. The defense always has a catcher who is suited up and communicating. For example, with a runner starting at first base, the offense sacrifice bunts on the first-base side to move the runner to second (figure 6.13). They then attempt a drag bunt to move the runner to third. Finally, they perform a safety squeeze to advance the runner home. Each bunt play is signaled by the third-base coach, so the players are getting the signs reinforced. All movement on the bases is full speed, and the defense is trying to defend the bunts.

Variations

1. To make this drill more challenging for the defense, a throw-down first base can be placed at 85 feet (25.9 m) instead of 90 feet (27.4), which requires the defense to play at a faster speed to record an out.
2. To make this drill more challenging for the offense, tell the bunters that they have two strikes on them. With two strikes, they have one attempt to execute the bunt. A point system is a great way to make the drill more competitive. Points are awarded for each base advanced, and double points are awarded for scoring a run before the defense records three outs.

Figure 6.13 Bunter executes a sacrifice bunt with a runner on first base while the pitcher defends the bunt.

3. Another twist is to divide the offense into two teams that compete against each other. The pitchers are on defense, and a catch net is in place of the catcher. Each team has nine outs to get on base, advance runners, and score runners with the bunt. Whichever team scores the most runs wins.

Coaching point

One thing is to be aware of when you play small game is to set up cones or discs at the defenders' normal positions and require them to play there. They are not allowed to cheat although they know that every play is a bunt play.

Common errors and corrections

The biggest error is the bunter running out of the box too soon. Remind the bunters that placement is more important than getting out of the batter's box quickly. Also, batters frequently bunt the ball too hard. Emphasize to the bunters that they must bunt the ball off the end of the bat to deaden the ball.

CHAPTER 7

Aggressive Baserunning

Aggressive and intelligent baserunning is as much of a run-scoring factor as hitting. With the exception of the home run that leaves the ballpark, baserunning is what scores runs.

Jerry Weinstein, former head baseball coach at Sacramento City College and current manager of the Modesto Nuts in the California League

Baserunning is one of the six weapons mentioned in chapter 2 that a high-scoring offense uses to attack the defense and score runs. "Baserunning can help win or lose more games than any other phase of the offense," according to Rich Alday, former head baseball coach for the University of New Mexico.

After the batter swings the bat, he becomes a base runner. Great base runners have the ability to advance themselves. Andy Lopez, head baseball coach at the University of Arizona, tells his base runners not to live the myth that it is the batter's job to propel the runner around the bases. Instead, aggressive and intelligent base runners can advance themselves without the aid of the hitter. The high-scoring offense takes pride in runners getting themselves around the bases.

Getting on base does not necessarily win games; getting *around* the bases is what wins games. Although many players think that good baserunning is reserved for the base stealers, aggressive baserunning by every team member is a requirement of the high-scoring offense. Essentially, a base runner has one responsibility—to do everything possible to score. Aggressive and smart base runners put pressure on the opposition, which can cause the defense to throw to the wrong base or make a rushed throw. As a result, the base runner can take the extra base.

Every player can be a good base runner regardless of the position that he plays or his running ability. The key to being a good base runner is to be prepared for everything that can happen. If you are well prepared, you will make proper decisions without hesitation. If you are not well prepared, indecision will make you miss many opportunities to advance. As a base runner you have the opportunity to turn the momentum of the game. The well-prepared base runner recognizes opportunities quickly and takes advantage of them. The attitude of an intelligent and aggressive base runner is that he wants to score runs, to take the extra base, and to run.

Good teams are often judged by their ability to manufacture runs. They do not rely solely on their ability to string hits together to score runs. Instead, they use other offensive weapons, such as aggressive baserunning, to maximize the efforts of the offense. Poor baserunning will inhibit a team's ability to manufacture runs on a regular basis and is a rally killer. The opposite is also true: Good baserunning can create and prolong rallies.

"Inches and seconds. Games are won or lost by a few inches or fraction of a second," according to Mark Johnson, former head coach at Texas A&M. A brief hesitation, a turn too wide, an arcing path—these and many other practices can cause a team to lose by an inch or second. A base runner who can run to first in 4.5 seconds covers 2 feet (60 cm) every 10th of a second. Countless base runners have been safe or out by less than 2 feet, or a 10th of a second.

Base runners must have an aggressive plan on each pitch. They must understand that running straight lines, taking proper angles, recognizing and reacting properly to the ball after it leaves the pitcher's hand, and fighting for inches all play an important role in helping the base runner get himself around the bases in a timely and efficient manner.

Base runners need to know how to run the bases intelligently and aggressively with the proper mindset: They shouldn't rely on the batter to get the runner around the diamond, but rather move themselves forward and, ultimately, score. Each base has its own set of rules and techniques that makes a base runner more proficient. The checklists in this chapter provide useful tips and coaching points to help the base runner get from one base to another.

HOME TO FIRST

Aggressive base runners always run their best time to first base. Sadly, some players seem incapable of running all out for 90 feet (27.4 m), an event that takes a little over four seconds and happens at most four or five times per game. Casual fans frequently see major-league players not giving their best effort running to first base, especially when they assume that they are going to be out. This practice sets a bad example for amateur players. Several years ago, the Oakland Athletics showed the entire organization a film clip of New York Yankees shortstop Derek Jeter giving his best effort running down the first-base line. This event was significant because the video was from about 130 games into the season, the Yankees were in first place, and at that point they had the game in hand. Jeter still ran his best time (4.2) to first. He is the consummate professional and the type of player whom the Athletics want to emulate—a player who runs the bases hard 100% of the time.

Aggressive base runners are always looking to take the extra base. In his first plate appearance in the first game of the championship series versus Fresno State at the 2008 College World Series, Ryan Peisel of the University of Georgia hit a routine single to left. When the left fielder did not crash hard to get the ball, Peisel never stopped running and took second base. This phenomenal play made a statement that Georgia was going to be aggressive. One of the hallmarks of an aggressive attacking offense is a team that runs hard to first base and makes aggressive turns at first. They never concede the next base. They are always looking for a mishandled ball, an open base, or a poorly thrown ball that will allow them to take an extra base.

Joe Madden, manager of the Tampa Bay Rays, demands just one thing of his players—always to give their best effort running to first base. He believes that if he can get his players to do that one thing, their effort and attention to detail will be at a high level in all areas of the game.

1. Lead with your back foot.
2. Find the ball immediately.
3. On a ground ball that stays in the infield, run in a straight line through first base.
   a. Look at first base and focus on the feet of the first baseman. This practice helps you to adjust your steps so that you can touch the front edge of the base and allows you to observe the feet of the first baseman should you need to avoid a tag at the last second (figure 7.1).
   b. Slide only to avoid bad throws, which will usually be thrown up the line and cause the first baseman to come toward home plate.
4. Break the tape just like a sprinter finishing a race. You should have a forward body lean when you touch the front edge of the base (figure 7.2). Never leap or jump at the base.
5. After touching the front of the base, peek over your right shoulder to check for an overthrow (figure 7.3).
6. Break down by shortening your steps, lowering your center of gravity, and widening your feet. At the completion of breaking down you should look over your left shoulder for an opening at second base (figure 7.4). An opening is created when second base is uncovered because the shortstop backhanded a ball in the six hole and overthrew the first baseman and the second baseman is backing the play up. The pitcher is watching the play, and no one is covering second base. This opportunity can be a game changer if you can recognize it and take the open base.
7. After you recognize that the ball gets through the infield, you should immediately start your turn into first base. Think double all the way and remember that you are no longer a hitter after you make contact.
   a. As a rule, after you recognize that the ball is going into the outfield, you need to head immediately toward the coach's box, which is 20 feet (6.1 m) down from first base and 15 feet (4.6 m) off the line. This location serves as the pivot point to make your turn into first base.
   b. Drive your outside arm across your body to keep from swinging out toward right-center field on the turn.
   c. Drop your inside shoulder and your eyes before touching the base and hit the inside second-base side of the first-base bag, which catapults you toward second.
   d. You can hit the base with either foot. Look at the base as you touch it and then pick up the outfielder.

Figure 7.1 Base runner approaches first base staring at the front edge of the bag and observing the feet of the first baseman.

Figure 7.2 Base runner touches front edge of the base with either foot, combined with a forward body lean.

Figure 7.3 Breaking down, looking right for an overthrow.

Figure 7.4 Looking left for an opening (second base uncovered).

e. When you touch the bag you should be in a straight line with second and return to the bag only when the outfielder has secured the baseball and forces you to stop.

f. After you have determined that you cannot advance, keep your eyes on the ball as you return to the base. If the ball is in right field, the turn will be shorter, and you should return to the base facing the fielder with the ball.

8. After you round first base, use two sideways shuffles at the completion of your turn instead of coming to an abrupt stop. You shuffle just as you do when taking a secondary lead, reading the outfielder to ensure that he secures the ball and throws it into second properly. You then stop and return to first base. After you return to the base touch the bag with your left foot, spin, open up, and find the ball. Be ready to run in case the ball gets away from one of the fielders.

9. When returning to first base on a ball hit from left-center field to the left-field line, you should turn toward the infield. When the ball is hit from the left-center-field gap to the right-field line, open up toward the outfield to return to first.

10. An average major-league player runs to first base from the right side of the box in 4.3 seconds and from the left side in 4.2 seconds. The stopwatch starts when the ball is hit and stops when the runner touches the bag. Your time should not deviate more than 0.3 second when you make an efficient turn.

RUNNER ON FIRST BASE

As a runner at first base, you will make most decisions according to the situation. You must know the score, the number of outs, the pitcher's tendencies, the catcher's tendencies, the positioning of each defensive player, the type of hitter, the ability of each runner in front of you, and, most of all, your own ability. All this information will help you make good decisions.

You must do three things after you reach base at the completion of the play. First, you must repeat the number of outs to the third-base coach with your hands (figure 7.5). Second, you must get the sign from the third-base coach, and third, you must put your head on a swivel and check the defensive positioning (figure 7.6). At that point you can take your lead.

Checklist: Runner on First

1. Do not make the first or last out at third base.

2. Always vault back to the base on a head-high line drive in the infield, with the exception of a line drive to first if the first baseman is holding you on.

3. Running lanes, in or out, depend on where the first baseman is playing. Take the throwing lane away from the first baseman on a ground ball or pickoff throw.

4. Always slide into second base if a play is being made on you.

5. The only time that you need a coach is when the ball is hit to the right of the right fielder. Pick up the third-base coach if the ball is hit from the right fielder to the right-field line. You should look at the third-base coach when you are approximately halfway, about 45 feet (13.7 m) from first base, or when you are about even with the pitcher's mound.

Figure 7.5 Runner gives outs back to coach with both hands.

Figure 7.6 Runner scans outfield to determine fielder placement.

6. On fly balls, go as far as the ball is hit and tag on all fly balls that are foul.

7. The number one priority of the runner at first base is to go first to third on a single.

8. If no play is on, you should never get picked off. Also, never get picked on a hit-and-run, delay steal, bunt, or a 3-1 or 3-2 count pitch.

9. In a first-and-third situation, never run into a tag at second base before the runner at third base has a chance to score.

10. When the ball is in the outfield, take a good aggressive shuffle and force the defense to get the ball in quickly. Challenge the defense to field the ball cleanly and make good throws.

Primary Lead

Before taking a primary lead, you must make sure that the pitcher has the ball. You are focused on the pitcher while taking your lead and never look back toward first base. You should get your primary lead before the pitcher gets set. Take the lead from back half of the bag. This positioning helps you stay in a straight line to second when you cross over to run to second base. The safe primary lead should be 9 feet (2.7 m), meaning that your right foot is on the 9-foot mark (figure 7.7). Start with the right foot and take two more steps to get out to 9 feet. There is little chance of getting picked on the crossover because you are so close to the base. You should have your knees slightly bent and slightly wider than shoulder-width apart. Your weight is on the balls of your feet. The right foot is back and slightly open, and the hands are in an athletic position, not on knees.

Secondary Lead

After attaining your primary lead, your secondary lead starts when the pitcher's front foot lands. At the completion of the two shuffles the ball should be in the hitting zone. This lead should take you right to the edge of the safety zone (figure 7.8), which is 22 feet (6.7 m). This distance is the maximum secondary lead that most runners can achieve. If contact is made on the ground or in the air above the heads of the infielders, you cross over and react. If no contact is made, then the first step has to be hard back toward first base.

Dirt Ball Reads

To execute a dirt ball read properly, the aggressive base runner breaks before the ball hits the ground. The premise is that the catcher is going to his knees

Figure 7.7 Primary lead, 9 feet off first base.

Figure 7.8 Secondary lead, edge of safety zone, 22 feet off first base.

to block the ball and that he will not have enough time to get up and throw out the runner advancing to the next base. Base runners who are good at anticipating the ball in the dirt do their homework before they get on first base. They pay close attention to the game to determine in which counts breaking balls are being thrown. An aggressive base runner must be able to read balls in the dirt from his regular secondary lead as well as a fake break. This skill is especially important for players who are not base stealers because it gives them a way to advance themselves without stealing a base.

Advancing on a dirt ball is just as good as a stolen base because the team is getting an extra base without giving up anything. Everyone on the ballclub should be proficient at advancing on a ball in the dirt. The goal is to eliminate hesitation. The runner does this by focusing on the pitcher's release. By the time the ball gets three-quarters of the way to plate, he decides whether the ball is in the dirt or not. If the pitch is moving at a downward angle and is in the dirt, the runner takes second base; if the ball is up, he shifts his eyes to contact and reacts accordingly.

RUNNER ON SECOND BASE

Knowing the positioning of the defense is more important when you are on second base because more balls will be hit behind you. By knowing where the defensive players are positioned you can make most of your decisions without having to turn around and wait for the play to develop. The depth of the lead is determined by the number of outs. With no outs you are in a straight line with third. With two outs you take two steps straight back of the base line to facilitate the turn at third base in the event of a base hit. Know your verbal commands from the coach and what they mean. For example, "OK" means take another step, "Careful" means stop, and "Back" means exactly that. You need to keep your eyes on the pitcher when taking your lead. The coach is responsible for not letting the runner get too far off the bag and learning which runners can react quickly and which ones are slower to react.

Checklist: Runner on Second

1. With less than two outs when you are the only runner on base at second, you should never advance to third until you see the ball pass the pitcher on the ground and not hit firmly in front of him.

2. Vault back on all head-high line drives.

3. When advancing to third, slide feet first, not headfirst. The feet-first slide allows you to get up more quickly and score if the ball gets by the third baseman.

4. Understand the halfway principal. With less than two outs on a fly ball you read the ball from the halfway mark, or the point halfway between your secondary lead and the base. Do not read the fly ball from the base. The halfway principal allows you to take a few steps back to touch the base, tag, and go to the next base or to score from the halfway mark if the ball falls.

5. Check the positioning of the outfielders by rotating your head back and forth like a windshield wiper. Do your homework.

6. On a ground ball hit at you, go.

7. Run on the swing with two strikes and two outs.

8. Never make either the first or second out at the plate.

9. With two outs when attempting to score from second base on a base hit, you must run full out through home plate to ensure that you score in the event that the batter gets thrown out at second.

10. A tight turn when rounding third base could mean the difference between a run scored and an out.

Primary Lead and Secondary Lead

The same rules apply at second base as at first base when taking your primary and secondary lead. The difference is in the distance of each and the increased reaction time in responding to the pitcher's pickoff move. The distance of the primary, non-stealing lead is 17 feet (5.2 m) (figure 7.9). Start with your right foot and takes five steps followed by one sideways shuffle, bringing your left foot to your right foot and resetting your feet. The secondary lead at second base is 29 feet (8.9 m) (figure 7.10). This aggressive secondary lead must be practiced, but it will ultimately lead to more runs scored. We have all seen runners get thrown out at the plate on bang-bang plays. A better jump and a better lead increase the odds of being safe.

Figure 7.9   The primary, non-stealing lead at second base is 17 feet.

Figure 7.10   The secondary lead at second base is 29 feet.

Five Ways to Get to Third Base on a Ground Ball

A runner at second base in a nonforce situation must be able to react properly to balls put in play on the infield in terms of whether to stay at second or advance to third base. One of the most embarrassing outs in baseball is getting thrown out trying to advance to third base on a ball hit back to the pitcher. To avoid this embarrassment, runners need to know when to go and when not to. Coaches should simulate and practice the five following ground ball scenarios frequently.

1. A slow roller to third base is an automatic *go*.
2. Past pitcher, left of shortstop, *go*.
3. Shortstop and third baseman cross; third baseman moves to his left, *go*.
4. Shortstop leaves the dirt and comes in on the grass to field the ball, *go*.
5. Shortstop in six hole, *go* on release. React to what you see. Second baseman should cover the bag.

RUNNER ON THIRD BASE

There are three basic reads at third base with less than two outs. The first is with the infield back, and the second two are with the infield in.

Infield Back

The first read is with a runner at third base, the infield back, no outs, and no force at the plate. The rule here is to go home on a ground ball when it is past the pitcher and not to third. The runner reads the ground ball and breaks for home after it gets by the pitcher or is hit to the first baseman playing back. But if the ball is hit back to the pitcher or directly at the third baseman, he must stay at third. The key here is first to read the direction of the ball and then to make the decision to run. The base runner vaults back to third on all head-high line drives. He tags on all fly balls in fair or foul territory, with the exception of a Texas Leaguer, which is a shallow fly ball just over the heads of the infielders. On this ball the runner goes halfway down the line and reads the ball. If it falls in he goes home; if it is caught he goes back to third. He does not tag because the ball is not hit deep enough.

Infield In, One Out

The second read is with the infield in and one out, no force play, and the infield playing up to prevent the run from scoring on a ground ball. The runner breaks for home on contact regardless of the direction or speed of the ground ball. This extremely aggressive read eliminates hesitation. Remind the runner to run first and react second. If the ball is hit back to the pitcher and he fields it cleanly, the runner stops about three-quarters of the way to home plate and yells, "Rundown," so that the batter–runner knows that the runner at third is going to stay in a pickle long enough for him to get to second base. On any other ground ball the runner continues to home plate and slides feet first.

Checklist: Runner on Third

1. Know how many outs there are. The stakes are magnified because you are only 90 feet (27.4 m) from scoring a run.

2. Have a heightened awareness of the signs at third because of a possible squeeze, a contact play, or a first-and-third double steal.

3. On a single or a double to the outfield with other runners on base, you should try to get the bat and catcher's mask out of the way in case the next runner has to slide in around them. You also become a coach for the next runner possibly coming in. If there is any doubt, tell them to slide. Better to make this decision early than late.

4. On a squeeze bunt, break for home when the pitcher's stride foot lands or at release point.

5. If you get in a rundown on a contact play, stay in the rundown until the batter–runner can get to second base so that he is in scoring position. You should yell, "Rundown," to let the batter–runner know to go to second.

6. With the infield in and no outs, do not take a secondary lead because if a ground ball is hit to third you will get tagged out by the third baseman. With no outs and the infield in, you are making sure that ground balls and line drives go through.

7. With runners at first and third, if the ball is hit hard to the third baseman, go home immediately to try to entice the third baseman to throw home, which is a tougher double play to turn than the traditional 5-4-3 double play.

8. In a first-and-third situation do not go on a routine ball hit to the first baseman, third baseman, or pitcher. Wait to break until the defensive player throws the ball toward second.

9. When tagging up at third base always face the ball and use the side of the bag to push off. Push off with the left foot on balls hit from right center over and push off on the right foot when the ball is hit from the left-field line over.

10. Run on the inside of the third-base line toward home on all bunts.

If the ball is a line drive at an infielder, the runner will be out because he is breaking on contact. The true contact play affords the base runner at third with a great jump on a ground ball, which puts enormous pressure on the infielders to field the ball cleanly and make an accurate throw home. The disadvantage is the possibility of getting doubled off on a line drive.

On a fly ball the runner would stop his forward progress and return to the base to tag. The third-base coach would give a signal to the back runner to let him know to advance immediately to third on a ground ball because the offense is running on contact and there is no reason to hesitate when coming to third.

Infield In, No Outs

The last read occurs when the opposition plays the infield in with no outs and no force on the runner. This typically happens when the defense is behind late in the game and cannot afford to give up another run. In this situation the runner at third would take his normal four-step primary lead but would not take a secondary lead. This lead helps the runner get back on a line drive in the infield. The rule here on a ground ball is to see it through the infield before going home. The runner vaults back on all head-high line drives and tags on all fly balls, with the exception of a Texas Leaguer. With the infield in the defense is extremely vulnerable to the hard-hit ground ball and the shallow fly ball because of their loss in lateral range and positioning.

Primary and Secondary Leads

The primary lead is a four-step lead that starts in foul territory. Take your lead as close to the baseline as possible while staying in foul territory. The first step is with the right foot followed by three steps (left, right, left). Then square up to the baseline (figure 7.11). Take your lead in foul territory and return to the base in fair territory on all leads. Be sure to check the positioning of the third baseman each time that you return to the base because his position will ultimately determine the length of your lead. You must go back in to third base standing up to take the throwing lane away from the catcher.

The secondary lead is a right, left, right walking lead that starts when the pitcher's front foot lands. The key is to have the right foot land when the ball crosses the hitting area. The secondary lead is 21 feet (6.4 m) (figure 7.12). Make sure that your shoulders are square to the third-base line and that your right foot is at a 45-degree angle so that you can return to third if the hitter fails to make contact. You should reach a point where there is no delay in your progress when you are advancing on a ground ball. If the ball passes through the hitting area, take a crossover step into the baseline as you return to the base.

Figure 7.11 The primary lead from third base is a four-step lead in foul territory.

Figure 7.12 Secondary lead from third is a right-left-right walking lead that goes to 21 feet.

SEPARATORS

The following 10 principles are basic baserunning absolutes, nonnegotiable skills, that good base-running teams simply do not violate. They are called separators because they play a role in run scoring, but breaking one of the rules can derail the offense instantly by making the worst out in baseball—an out on the bases.

1. Always run with your head up and know where the ball is at all times. Never put your head down when running the bases. The only time that you should put your head down is to touch a base, and then you should immediately lift your head.

2. Never round the bag when the ball is in the infield.

3. Do what the runner ahead of you does.

4. Round the bag when the ball is in the outfield.

5. On a hit-and-run, make sure to look in to see where the ball is hit.

6. Know the base runner in front of you, especially if he is slow and you are fast so that you do not run up his back.

7. Never miss a signal.

8. On outfield throws, elevation and outs dictate what the trail runner does.

9. You can tag up at first base if there are less than two outs and the ball is likely to be caught. This is one of the best baserunning plays in baseball.

10. Always run hard crossing home plate because you never know about the trail runner.

THREE Ss OF THE ON-DECK BATTER

Your first responsibility as a base runner comes when you are in the on-deck circle. The on-deck hitter has three responsibilities that can assist his teammates. They are often overlooked but are potential game changers for the high-scoring offense.

Slash   The on-deck batter must keep his eyes on the shortstop and third baseman when a runner is at second and the bunt sign is given to the batter. If the on-deck batter observes the shortstop breaking for third and the third baseman crashing in the bunter's face, he should yell, "Slash!" The on-deck batter becomes the eyes of the hitter because he must concentrate on the pitch.

Steal   The on-deck batter should yell, "Take it," when he sees the base runner at first or second getting a great jump on a steal attempt. This instruction will prevent the batter from swinging at a pitch and fouling it off when the runner might have had the base stolen easily. This skill can be perfected during intrasquad games. The on-deck batter can also yell, "Pitchout," when he sees the catcher step out early.

Slide   The on-deck batter should always anticipate a play at the plate where his help is needed. When he gets to the plate area, he positions himself where the runner can easily see him, and he makes his decision early to let the runner know whether to slide or not. If there is any question, he should always have the runner slide. When signaling the runner to slide, the on-deck batter gets down on his knees and keeps his hands down. When signaling the runner to stay up, he stands up and holds his hands high above his head. A verbal command may cause confusion and should be avoided.

Base-Coaching Absolutes

1. With runners on base and less than two outs, the coach cannot let the runner at first base get doubled off on a line drive.

2. The coach should remind runners not to let the second baseman tag them on their way to second base with runners on. The base runner should fall down and roll away from the tagger or stop and retreat.

3. On steals or on a hit-and-run, the runner should be taught not to try to get back on line drives. He should just keep going because he cannot get back anyway.

4. Runners on their way to second must visually pick up the third-base coach halfway to second base on balls to right field (figure 7.13).

5. The coach predetermines sending the base runner home from second with two outs on a single. The third-base coach should alert the first-base coach so that the trail runner can go to second without stopping or hesitating.

6. The third-base coach should let base runners know that he is a stop sign only. He is not a go sign. This plan helps eliminate hesitation.

7. The coach points his hand at the third-base bag before the base runner takes his lead at first to remind him that he must go into third standing up with two outs if he is going to go two bases on a single.

8. When running from first to third base on a single to right field, base runners should remember the coach–base–coach rule. The runner looks at the third-base coach when he is halfway to second base for direction, looks down to touch the base, and then picks up the third-base coach again after he rounds second in case the coach changes his mind.

Figure 7.13 Runner picking up coach for sign at the halfway point.

9. The third-base coach should point to the ground down the third base line to tell the runner to round the bag to this point, find the ball, and take home in the event that the outfielder bobbles the ball.

10. When the third-base coach is behind third toward the outfield, the runner knows that he is scoring and that the coach is focused on the trail runner. When the coach is down the third-base line, the lead runner knows that he must watch the coach and obey his hand signals.

DRILLS

Following are three drills, in three completely different settings, to enhance baserunning skills. The first provides an array of ways to incorporate base running practice during BP. The second gives some baserunning rules for intra-squad games to promote aggressive baserunning. The final drill can be used both indoors or out and challenges base runners' ability to react intelligently to various situations.

Baserunning During Batting Practice

1. Decide how many groups you will have, usually three or four.
   a. Example: 45-minute BP with three groups at 15 minutes each.
   b. One group hits, one group plays defense, and one group does baserunning.

2. The group that is doing baserunning does 10 minutes wherever you want them to. The BP pitcher throws from the stretch to simulate a game. After 10 minutes, the base runners come in for 5 minutes of soft toss to get ready to hit.

3. The guys on defense go to baserunning, and the hitters go to defense.

4. Base runners can spend three minutes at each base. They take a five-step reaction on balls put in play.

5. During BP, teach going on contact at third base. Have players parallel with the third-base line. They practice reacting to the ball properly. If the ball is hit back to the L-screen, they yell, "Rundown." If contact is made on ground, players take five hard steps toward home. If no contact is made, players take one hard step into fair territory and look to see where the third baseman is.

6. Place a screen halfway down the third-base line to protect your players during the drill.

Intrasquad Games

Mandate that runners go two bases on all singles to the outfield. This directive promotes quick reads and potentially more runs, whereas delayed reads result in only one-base advancement and no runs. The goal is to eliminate hesitation. This approach also helps outfielders because they know that they have to be aggressive on every ball. Hitters have to read the lead runner. They know that a throw is going somewhere every time, so they must run hard out of box to get to second base if the outfielder makes a bad decision.

Aggressive base runners anticipate bad throws from outfielders. They do two things to help them read potential errant throws. First, they read the position of the cutoff man to determine whether he is in the proper place. The runner should know the target to which the outfielder is throwing. He should be able to read whether the ball is going to be offline or will short-hop the infielder on the relay. Second, the runner should read the arc of the ball out of the hand of the outfielder in the first 10 feet (3 m) of the throw. The runner should know exactly where the throw is going: Is it offline? Is it high? Did the outfielder make a bad decision?

Reads and Reactions at First Base

Three runners at a time take their primary leads at first base. The coach faces the runners in the infield to start the drill. The purpose of the drill is to challenge the runners to make quick, intelligent decisions without hesitation. The coach yells, "Skip," and the runners take their secondary leads, getting out to the 22-foot (6.7 m) secondary lead boundary marked with a cone. The runners then react to the following coach's hand signals:

Read: One hand above the head is a Texas Leaguer (figure 7.14).

Reaction: The runners go halfway and respond to the coach who says, "Catch" or "Drop."

Figure 7.14 Texas Leaguer.

(continued) ⟹

Reads and Reactions at First Base *(continued)*

Read: Two hands above the head indicates a fly ball (figure 7.15).

Reaction: Runners get off first as far as possible, listening to the coach and returning when he claps his hands to indicate a catch.

Figure 7.15 Fly ball.

Read: A karate-chop motion across the chest back toward first base indicates a head-high line drive behind the runner (figure 7.16).

Reaction: Players run in response to a line drive hit behind them. They have no reason to vault back in this situation because if the first baseman catches the ball the runner is out regardless.

Figure 7.16 Head-high line drive behind runner.

Read: A karate-chop motion across chest toward second base indicates a head-high line drive in front of the base runner (figure 7.17).

Reaction: The runner vaults back immediately and then reacts to the coach's verbal command of "Catch" or "Through."

Figure 7.17   Head-high line drive in front of runner.

Read: The hand goes toward the ground in the direction of first to indicate a ground ball hit to the first baseman (figure 7.18).

Reaction: The runner breaks immediately for second and takes the throwing lane away from the first baseman.

Figure 7.18   Ground ball to first.

(continued) ➡

Reads and Reactions at First Base *(continued)*

Read: The hand goes down toward second to simulate a ground
             ball in front of the runner (figure 7.19).

Reaction: The runner breaks for second base immediately.

Figure 7.19   Ground ball in front of runner.

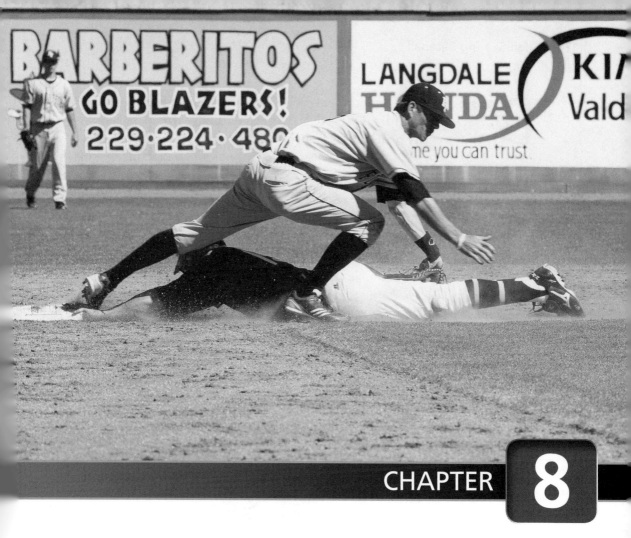

CHAPTER **8**

Intelligent Base Stealing

I gave the team a spark by reaching first base on a single or sometimes a walk. With my stolen-base ability, those singles and walks quickly became doubles and just like that we had a runner in scoring position.

Lou Brock, former St. Louis Cardinals outfielder and Hall of Famer

Base stealing is an important aspect of run scoring in baseball. In 1987 the St. Louis Cardinals speedster Vince Coleman "scored 23% of his 121 runs with no hit coming from his teammates after he reached base" (Will, 1990). Base stealing can be a significant part of manufacturing runs not only by getting runners into scoring position to score on a base hit but also, as Coleman did, by being able to score without the aid of a hit.

The value of a stolen base depends on the game situation and the runner's success rate.

> *The break-even point for the stolen base is highly dependent on the inning and score. The most desirable situations are tied games in the later innings or ones in which the batting team is ahead. The least desirable situations are down by at least two runs in the later innings. (Tango, Lichtman, & Dolphin, 2007)*

A base runner's strategy on the bases will depend on the inning, the number of outs, the score, and the pitcher's ability to control the running game. In short, a base stealer must always be aware of the value of stealing and the effect that a stolen base will have on the team's ability to score a run.

> *With a man on first, and no one else on, the team is expected to score .953 runs with no outs. If the runner gets to second, and all other things are equal, that run expectancy is now 1.189, or a positive change of .236 runs . . . . An out would turn the .953 run situation into a .297 run situation, or a net loss of .656 runs. (Tango, Lichtman, & Dolphin, 2007)*

Even the threat of stealing a base can wreak havoc with the opposing pitcher, catcher, and infielder covering the bag and the coach relaying signs or pickoff plays.

> *A base runner who is a potential base stealer has a tremendous adverse effect on the pitcher. It divides his attention. The base runner also has a great effect on the defense. It takes them out of character and makes them do things they haven't practiced. The third baseman is pulled in, and the middle infielders may be jockeying a runner on second base to keep him close. All these things contribute to creating larger holes in the infield for the hitter to hit through.*
>
> Maury Wills, former major-league shortstop

The pitcher must now divide his attention between the batter and the base runner close to the base. The pitcher will probably throw more fastballs to give the catcher a better opportunity to throw out the would-be base stealer. In addition, whenever a middle infielder is covering second base on a steal attempt, the hitter has an open hole in the infield to drive the baseball through. The threat of a stolen base creates pressure that can be measured.

"A runner on first base with less than two outs is an enormous disruption on the defense. The batter gains 14 points on his wOBA (weighted on-base average)" (Tango, Lichtman, & Dolphin, 2007).

A successful steal attempt moves the base runner either into scoring position at second base, eliminating the biggest rally killer in baseball (the double play), or to third base, where he can score without the aid of a base hit. It is all a matter of risk versus reward. "From 1999 to 2002 the steal success rate against RHPs in MLB was 66.4% and 58.7% versus LHPs" (Tango, Lichtman, & Dolphin, 2007). Knowledge, technique, and practice will allow a base stealer to increase his success rate. "In the eighth and later innings the break-even point hovers around 65%. And in these innings, teams were actually successful 69% of the time" (Tango, Lichtman, & Dolphin, 2007). Good base stealers have adequate speed, use proper technique, and study the pitcher for clues that will give them a head start. To steal a base, the base runner must get a good jump in his first several steps toward the next base. The lead that he takes off the base is also important. He must fight for inches but also feel comfortable that he can return to the base on a pickoff attempt by the pitcher. Each base stealer is striving for the maximum lead that will allow him to return safely as well as get his best jump on a steal attempt.

The ability to steal a base depends on time and distance. The time required for a base stealer to go from his lead off first base, travel the distance to second, and perform his slide into the base must be less than the time needed for the pitcher to deliver the baseball to the plate, for the catcher to throw to second base, and for the infielder to apply the tag. The use of the stopwatch is critical in estimating the chances that the base stealer will be safe. The opposing pitcher should be timed from his first action toward home plate from the stretch position, such as when the heel of his lead foot leaves the ground, until the baseball makes contact with the catcher's mitt. Most pitchers complete this action in 1.1 to 1.5 seconds.

The catcher must also be timed from when the baseball touches his glove until the middle infielder catches the baseball. An average time for a catcher is 2.0 seconds, commonly known as his pop time. Add an additional 0.1 second for the tag and then add the total together. For example, if the pitcher is 1.35 to the plate, the catcher is 2.0 to second base, and 0.1 second is added for the tag, then the total time would be 3.45 seconds. Each player should be timed at practice from his first move at his steal lead until he slides into second base. When a player knows his steal time and the combined time for the pitcher and catcher to second, then he is equipped with all the information that he needs to determine whether the risk to steal a base is advantageous. A good base stealer will attempt to steal only when he has his best jump. Exceptional base stealers have a green light, meaning that they can steal whenever they get their best jump. Of course, if the coach gives the must-steal sign, then the base runner must attempt to steal regardless of his jump.

STEALING SECOND BASE

The first three things that a base runner should do after reaching base are to know the number of outs, get the sign from the coach, and scan the entire outfield and infield to know the positioning of the fielders. Additionally, the runner should make a mental note of the score and the inning. All this information is collectively known as the checklist. The information gleaned while completing the checklist will help the base runner eliminate indecision on the base paths.

When attempting a stolen base the base runner must get to his minimum steal lead at first base, which should be between 13 and 15 feet (4 and 4.6 m) off the bag. The base runner should toe the back edge of the bag with his left foot and extend his lead in a straight line. This lead allows him to dive back into the corner of the bag farthest from the first baseman's attempt to apply a tag on a pickoff. Similarly, a base runner should slide into the back edge of the base that he is advancing to because it is farther from the catcher's throw and the tag attempt by the infielder.

The base runner needs to get his minimum steal lead under control quickly. Most base stealers take their lead before or while the pitcher is getting the sign from the catcher. The base runner should take two steps, right then left, while facing second base, keeping his eyes on the pitcher. This lead allows the base runner to go back into first base standing up if an immediate pickoff is attempted. After taking these first two steps, the base runner should pivot so that his shoulders are square to the baseline and then move to his minimum steal lead by taking two slide steps, moving the right foot first and then bringing the left foot to but not crossing over the right foot. This sideways progression puts the base runner in a position to react to an attempted pickoff. After establishing the lead, the base runner should assume an athletic stance that has the feet slightly wider than the shoulders, the weight on the balls of the feet, both arms hanging loosely in front of the body, the knees slightly flexed, and the right foot slightly open and dropped back a few inches (about 10 cm) from parallel with the left foot (figure 8.1). While extending the lead, the runner's eyes stay on the pitcher. When the pitcher has the baseball he is the only person who can pick off the base runner.

After the base runner has completed his minimum steal lead, he should dive back into the back corner of first base if a pickoff is attempted. This technique for diving back into first base is called one step and a dive. The runner takes a crossover step with his right foot toward the back edge of the base, extending his left arm toward the ground (figure 8.2a). The runner should use the spoke technique when his left hand hits the ground to avoid injury to the fingers on his left hand on the dive back. The fingers of the left hand must not go straight into the ground. Instead, the fingers should be closed

Figure 8.1 Minimum steal lead is between 13-15 feet from the back edge of the bag with an athletic stance, feet slightly wider than shoulder width apart, and weight on balls of feet with arms hanging loosely.

(mitten style), the wrist should be rotated slightly back toward the outfield side of the bag, and the thumb and fingertips should form a kind of bridge when planted on the dirt. The pressure of the landing will be absorbed by the V between the thumb and fingers, which will prevent the fingers from being bent backward. The base runner must dive back, staying low and making sure that his chest hits the ground first, not his knees. The base runner then reaches with his right hand and slides into the back edge of the base (figure 8.2*b*). The base runner must remember to turn his head toward the outfield when diving back, ensuring that an errant throw by the pitcher will hit him in the back of the helmet rather than the face.

After diving back into first base the base runner should always keep his right hand on the base (figure 8.2*c*), walk his left foot up to his right hand, and step on first base. By using this technique the base runner maintains constant contact with the base so that the first baseman cannot tag him out when he has possession of the baseball. The base runner must find the baseball as soon as he stands up. After the first baseman throws the baseball back to the pitcher, the runner can proceed to his minimum steal lead. The idea is to get a lead quickly and under control each time. This up-tempo style helps make the pitcher uncomfortable and allows the base stealer to establish his minimum steal lead without getting quick pitched. Too often, base runners are too conservative with their leads off first base, which results in their getting thrown out at second base more frequently. Emphasize to potential base stealers that being picked off at first base is better than being thrown out at second base.

After the base runner is at his minimum steal lead, he needs to create some momentum before taking his first step toward second base. Establishing momentum can be accomplished in several ways. One technique is for the

Figure 8.2 *(a)* Diving back into first, beginning to use crossover step with right foot. *(b)* Left-hand "spoke" technique to avoid injury on dive back, with head turned away from pitcher and right hand touching the back corner of the bag. *(c)* The runner must maintain contact with the base.

base runner to descend slowly with the upper body while he is at his steal lead coiling the body for momentum. Another involves inverting the right knee (figure 8.3). Establishing momentum allows a quicker start because a body in motion can react faster than a stationary one (figure 8.4).

Getting a good jump is critical to becoming an exceptional base stealer. To be able to get a good jump, the base runner must be able to read the pitcher's move. He can do this by getting an extended one-way lead. A one-way lead is the maximum lead from which the base runner can safely return to the base. The purpose of a one-way lead is to give the runner insight into the pitcher's move and, ideally, to entice him into using his best move. The base runner can accomplish this without worrying about getting picked off because he is concerned only with diving back to the bag, not stealing.

After the base runner has seen the pitcher's best move to first, he knows how far to extend his maximum lead. The moment that the base runner attempts to steal second base, his first step should be with his left foot in a crossover move, taking a straight line directly toward the outfield side of

Figure 8.3 Inverting lead knee to create momentum.

Figure 8.4 Base stealer breaking toward second base, staying low and not losing momentum.

the second-base bag. All good base stealers get going quickly within the first four to six steps. The base runner must keep his head level and not raise up, because raising up causes him to lose his momentum toward the second-base bag. After the base stealer has taken his third step, he should peek or glance toward home plate, where the baseball has reached the contact area. This glance is important because if the batter does not take the pitch and puts the ball in play, the base stealer must react accordingly. The principle behind this move is that the base runner should know where the ball is at all times. With practice, this peeking action should not impede the base stealer's running time to second base.

Players should understand that when stealing a base they will never get to full speed. They need to be reminded of this so that they can accelerate into their slide at second base. When attempting to steal, the base runner should continue only when he gets his best jump. Base runners need to choke off their steal attempt within two steps if they do not get their best jump. Players need to practice this advanced skill regularly so that they learn the difference between a good jump and their best jump.

Sliding headfirst into a base is the fastest way to get there. Headfirst sliding, however, is also the most dangerous way to slide into a base. For this reason, some players shy away from sliding headfirst. Sliding feet first has the advantage of allowing the base stealer to pop up and move to the next base on an overthrow by the catcher.

Regardless of which slide he employs, the player should always slide to the outfield side of the base (figure 8.5). Again, sliding to the farthest corner of the bag allows the base runner an additional few inches to avoid a throw and tag, which can be the difference between being safe or out.

Figure 8.5 Sliding into the back of the bag.

Reading the Pickoff Move to First

The key to getting a good jump at first base is anticipation, relaxation, and knowledge of the pitcher. All good base stealers watch the opposing pitcher for clues that tip off whether he is picking to the base or delivering the baseball to home plate. The following are some basic clues that may telegraph whether the pitcher is picking to first base or delivering the ball to home plate.

Stealing Versus the Right-Handed Pitcher

Base runners can look for three keys to decide whether the pitcher is picking to first or delivering the ball to the plate.

Front Shoulder The first clue to reading a pitcher's pickoff move to first base is the pitcher's front shoulder. If the pitcher's front shoulder is open when he comes to the set position, he must close it down to deliver the baseball to home plate (figure 8.6). As soon as the pitcher turns his front shoulder toward home plate, the base stealer can break. Other pitchers may come set with their shoulders square to the plate, but when they decide to throw to the batter they cock the front shoulder before lifting the front heel. Also, lifting the chin can be a clue before the pitcher initiates the delivery with the front heel. Again, if the base stealer can pick up on the pitcher's "tells," he can start his jump and enhance his break by getting an early start toward second base.

Figure 8.6 Position of right-handed pitcher's front shoulder starting open.

Timing and Rhythm Additional factors in getting a good jump are timing and rhythm. A good base stealer develops an idea of the maximum number of consecutive picks that a pitcher will make before delivering the baseball to home plate. The base runner should also know whether the pitcher will attempt a pickoff while his hands are moving up or coming down toward the set position. The good base stealer also learns the time that elapses from when the pitcher comes set and when he picks or pitches to home plate. To do this, the base runner can use an ABCD analogy. He should start listing letters one second apart to learn whether the pitcher gets into a pattern of coming set and delivering the baseball to home plate on the same letter each time. If the

Figure 8.7 Right-handed pitcher lifting front heel, indicating when to steal.

pitcher delivers the baseball to home plate on the letter C (a three count) each time, then the base stealer can get a better jump by anticipating this scenario.

Reading the Front Foot The successful base stealer can focus his attention on the pitcher's front foot. As soon as the front foot moves (figure 8.7), the runner should take off. If the base stealer recognizes any other movement before the pitcher moves his front foot, he should anticipate a pickoff attempt. If a pitcher doesn't obviously display any of these three common tells, runners may have to look more closely. Along with his teammates and coaches in the dugout, the runner should start looking at the pitcher's head and then move down the pitcher's body, looking for any-thing that the pitcher may do to tip his hand before he lifts his front heel, which initiates his move to the plate.

Stealing Versus the Left-Handed Pitcher

When a runner is facing a left-handed pitcher (LHP) whom he has not seen before, he must assume that the pitcher has a good pickoff move. Base steal-ers should take a one-way lead and force the pitcher to show his best move. After learning the LHP's best move, runners can look for clues that the pitcher may use to tip off his pick to first base. Most LHPs predetermine in their mind whether they will attempt a pickoff or throw a pitch to the plate. After the LHP receives the sign from the catcher, he glances at the runner and has committed in his mind either to pitch the ball to the plate or to pick to first base. Most pitchers are focused on either picking to first base or executing their pitch instead of reacting quickly to whether the base runner is attempt-ing to steal or not.

Head The first clue to reading a LHP's pickoff move comes from the pitcher's head movement. After the pitcher comes set and lifts his front leg to its apex, the runner should focus on the pitcher's head. While the front leg is held high, if the pitcher is looking to home, he will throw to first (figure 8.8). Conversely, if the LHP is looking to first base, he will throw home. LHPs often fall into a pattern. After a base runner has figured out the pattern, he is able to get a better jump.

Figure 8.8 Left-handed pitcher at the apex of his leg lift looking home often indicates a pickoff attempt.

Upper Body Pitchers can give away their pickoff move by leaning with the upper body. After the pitcher comes set and lifts his front leg to its apex, the runner should focus on the LHP's upper body. If the pitcher leans back, he is going to pick to first base (figure 8.9). If the pitcher leans forward, he is going to deliver the baseball home.

Figure 8.9 When left-handed pitcher leans back with upper body, it may indicate a pickoff attempt to first base.

Lead Leg A third clue may be found in the pitcher's lead leg. When the lead leg reaches its apex, the runner should look to see whether his lead leg is turned back (closed). If the leg is closed, the pitcher intends to deliver the baseball home. If the lead leg is open slightly, the LHP will throw the baseball to first base (figure 8.10).

Figure 8.10 A slightly open leg may indicate a pick.

Hands and Legs A fourth indicator is in the hands and legs. If the pitcher moves his hands first he will go home (figure 8.11*a*); if he moves his lead leg first he will go to first base (figure 8.11*b*).

Figure 8.11 *(a)* Hands move first indicates pitch; *(b)* lead leg moves first indicates pick.

Unnatural Leg Lift The base runner should look for an unnatural leg lift whenever the pitcher is attempting to pick to first base (figure 8.12). Many pitchers will use a particular leg lift or vary the tempo of the leg lift when they pitch and use a different one when they pick to first base.

First Move

Finally, if a base stealer cannot pick up any clues about whether the pitcher is picking or delivering to the plate, he can gamble by taking off on the pitcher's first move. As previously stated, most pitchers have already determined whether they are throwing home or to first base.

Figure 8.12 Left-handed pitcher with an unnatural leg lift, indicating a pick to first.

Knowing this, a base stealer can take off for second base as soon as he sees movement from the pitcher's front foot.

If the pitcher delivers the baseball to home plate, the base stealer should easily steal the bag. If the base stealer takes off and the pitcher picks to first, then the base stealer should immediately get to the infield side of the second-base bag as he runs toward second base. While running toward the infield side of the bag, the base runner should try to get in line with the infielder's glove. This positioning makes it more difficult for the first baseman to make an accurate throw to the second-base bag because the base runner is in the same line as the throw. Many times the first baseman will throw the baseball into the outfield because he will attempt to throw the ball over the base runner running to second base. Most teams are good at getting an out in a rundown situation, so the runner should get to the inside of the baseline and follow the middle infielder's glove.

DRILLS FOR STEALING SECOND BASE

Base-stealing drills should begin with learning how to return safely and quickly to the bag. This practice will build the base stealer's confidence. He has to be confident in the length of his lead and his ability to return safely to the bag before he can ever steal a base.

Dive Backs on the Grass

All players line up on the right-field line and use the foul line as first base. The coach acts as the pitcher and either pretends to pick to first base or delivers the baseball home, without throwing a ball (figure 8.13). All players get a lot of repetitions diving back to first base and working on their steal jumps.

Figure 8.13 Dive backs on the grass.

Four Man (Stealing Second)

Set up three bases behind the first-base bag and put a coach on the pitcher's mound with a baseball. Another coach serves as a first baseman. Use spray paint to mark off 13-, 14- and 15-foot (4.0, 4.3, and 4.6 m) leads in the dirt. Base runners should be wearing helmets because a baseball is used in this live drill.

Four players simultaneously take their leads off their respective bases, and the coach either fakes a delivery to home plate or picks at first base. The idea is for players to understand how far they can get off first base and still return safely. This drill allows players to establish their minimum steal lead. In many cases, players will be able to extend their lead beyond 15 feet (4.6 m). Getting picked off is acceptable in this drill because players will figure out how far is too far.

Two Man (Stealing Second)

This drill is the same as Four Man except that only one base is set up behind the first-base bag and one base is set up behind the second-base bag in line with third base. This drill is also live, employing a pitcher, catcher, first baseman, and two middle infielders. The rule is that for every time the pitcher picks to first base, he must deliver two pitches to the plate.

The base stealers are getting jumps off a pitcher, while the catcher attempts to throw out runners at second and the middle infielders work on applying tags. This competitive drill allows runners to learn whether they are safe or out on the steal attempt. Players can often learn a great deal about base stealing when real consequences are attached.

STEALING THIRD BASE

As Carl Crawford of the Boston Red Sox said, "Manufacturing runs is important. . . . That's why stealing [third] is becoming a big thing, too." If a base runner can get to third base with none or one out, he has more ways to score than he did from second, primarily because a base hit is not needed.

The best time to steal third base is with one out in the inning. But the runner should attempt to steal third only if he has an extremely high probability of success. The base runner is already in scoring position at second base, so if he is tagged out while stealing third, he has squandered a good chance of scoring a run that inning.

Base stealers should be more aggressive against LHPs because, with their backs to the base runner, LHPs are usually slower to the plate than RHPs. Again, the base runner should study the pitcher before reaching second base so that he can answer three questions:

1. How many looks does the pitcher make to second base before delivering the baseball home? Does he look one time, two times, three times? Or does he mix up his looks? Essentially, what is his pattern?

2. What is the pitcher's tempo on his head looks? In other words, how much time does he take to look at the runner and then turn his head to pick up the target to pitch? Does he slowly move his head from second base to home, or is his tempo quick?

3. Is he a "lock on" guy? After taking his looks at the base runner, regardless of his pattern and tempo, does he obviously slow down and lock in on the target before delivery?

Answering these questions gives the base runner the knowledge necessary to steal third successfully. As with leads at first base, the base runner must run through the checklist. He must know the number of outs, get the sign from the third-base coach, and check the positioning of the outfielders and infielders. One difference in the checklist at second base is always to end by checking the shortstop a second time before proceeding. The shortstop will be behind the base runner and out of his line of sight after the lead is completed.

A steal lead at second base is also a measured lead of 21 feet (6.4 m) or seven steps (versus 13 to 15 feet [4.0 to 4.6 m] taken at first base). The runner should start by toeing the back of the second-base bag with his left foot and walking seven steps, beginning with his right foot. After the runner has completed a seven-step lead, he should make a mark with his right foot. This mark enables him to return to the lead position without having to mark the leadoff every time.

After the base runner gets his seven-step lead, he extends his lead an additional 3 feet (.9 m) while the catcher is putting down the signs by simply slide stepping his left foot to his right foot, resetting his feet. The base runner is then 24 feet (7.3 m) from second base, marking the minimum steal lead.

From the minimum steal lead, the base runner can take two steps and a dive on a pickoff attempt. He crosses over with his right foot, steps with his left foot, uses the spoke technique with his left hand, and dives to the back of the second-base bag. At all times, the base runner must keep his eyes on the pitcher and listen to the third-base coach. If the base runner hears nothing from the coach, he is free to steal third base. If the third-base coach says, "Back one," the base runner must retreat 3 feet (.9 m) back to the 21-foot (6.4 m) mark. Depending on what the middle infielders do, the third-base coach can say, "OK," meaning that the base runner can return to the 24-foot (7.3 m) mark, the minimum lead from which he can attempt a steal of third base.

After the pitcher has made his last look to second base and turns his head toward home, the base runner takes a short (3 feet [.9 m]), quick sideways shuffle toward third base known as a vault (figure 8.14). When executing a vault, the hips and shoulders must remain square to the baseline and not open up prematurely. Maintaining the squared stance serves as a safety valve, allowing the base runner either to proceed to third or to return to second. The vault should be completed about a half second before the pitcher delivers the ball home. The key for the base runner is to vault when he cannot see one of the pitcher's eyes as the pitcher turns his head back to home the last time. If the pitcher's front leg moves, the runner should continue to third base with his head up and his eyes focused on the pitcher for a minimum of two steps. He does this because if the pitcher spins around toward second base after lifting his front leg, the base runner needs to stop and attempt to make it back to second base safely.

Figure 8.14 The base runner taking a short, quick, three-foot sideways shuffle (vault) toward third base.

After vaulting, if the pitcher does not deliver the baseball home, the base runner simply vaults back to his original 24-foot (7.3 m) lead. The base runner is then in a position to dive back to second base on a pickoff attempt or try to time the pitcher's head look again and vault.

The vault accomplishes two things. First, it allows the base runner to create momentum toward third base before the pitcher delivers the baseball home. Second, the vault is a safety valve if the pitcher lifts his front leg and spins in an attempt to pick the runner off second base. The base runner must practice the vault regularly so that he knows when he has established his best jump. Runners who get their best jump can continue toward third. Runners not achieving their best jump need to choke off the steal attempt within two steps and pull up.

DRILL FOR STEALING THIRD BASE

When doing drills to steal third base, coaches should encourage base stealers to be aggressive and anticipate the pitcher's head look back to the plate. The number one problem that base stealers have is that they hesitate, which makes them conservative and results in an inability to steal third base. Coaches should fall into patterns when serving as the pitcher in these drills so that players can recognize patterns and develop the ability to anticipate and get better jumps.

Four Man (Stealing Third)

Line up three bases behind second base in a straight line with the first-base bag. Paint lines at 21, 24, and 28 feet (6.4, 7.3, and 8.5 m). These lines represent where the base runner needs to be at each stage of his steal attempt of third base. One coach is on the pitcher's mound, and another coach is behind the four runners, serving as the third-base coach.

Four players each take a lead off one of the second bases. After the base runners take their 21-foot (6.4 m) leads, the coach on the mound looks toward home as if he is getting the sign from the catcher. From here, the base runners extend their leads to 24 feet (7.3 m) by taking a slide step and resetting their feet, listening to the coach behind them, and trying to time the pitcher's head looks. The base stealer will reach the 28-foot mark at the completion of his vault.

STEALING HOME

Stealing home can be accomplished only against a pitcher in the windup position whose delivery to the plate is slow. A slow windup is one that takes 3.2 seconds or longer to deliver the baseball to the plate.

Stealing home is an exciting but risky play; home is the most challenging base to steal. The base runner must start with a 24-foot (7.3 m) lead, or the equivalent of eight steps. The base runner must get to this lead quickly without drawing attention to himself. After he reaches this distance from third, the runner walks toward home plate. While walking, the runner should take three or more additional steps to have any chance of success. The base runner continues to walk toward home until the pitcher starts his windup.

After the pitcher starts his windup, the base runner takes off running toward home and slides feet first to prevent injury. If the pitcher looks at the base runner at any time, the runner should stop walking and get ready to return to the bag if the pitcher steps off the rubber. If the pitcher does not step off the rubber and looks home again, the base runner can resume walking. If the base runner does not get his three or more additional steps, he cannot break for home.

The coach must give the batter the take sign so that he will not swing if the base runner attempts to steal. The coach should provide no verbal cues to the runner. Any verbal cue could draw the pitcher's attention or attention from the opposing coaches in the dugout.

Stealing home is best attempted with two outs when the coach thinks that the batter has a poor chance of getting a hit.

DRILL FOR STEALING HOME

Attempting a steal of home with two strikes on the batter can be a way to score an important run. It worked for the University of Southern California in 1998 in the championship game of the College World Series. In the seventh inning, Morgan Ensberg "danced down the third-base line three times, bluffing like he was going to steal home. On a 1-2 count, he ran down the line again—and kept going. He slid safely, just under the tag, for a rare steal of home" (Horne, 1999). Coaches need to remember to give the batter the take sign.

Four Man (Stealing Home)

Line up three bases behind third base in a straight line with the second-base bag. Have a coach on the mound simulating a pitcher in the windup; no ball is needed.

All four base runners take an eight-step lead and walk toward home plate while the pitcher is getting his sign. Occasionally, the coach should look at the base runners or step off the rubber to make the simulation as gamelike as possible. This drill allows the coach to find out who has the aggressiveness and timing required to execute a theft of home plate.

CHAPTER **9**

Get 'Em On,
Get 'Em Over

To me, the secret of scoring a lot of runs is, as many times as you can get a guy in scoring position, do it. (Will, 1990)

Tony La Russa, former major-league manager and three-time World Series champion

This chapter focuses on strategies of how to get runners on base and how to advance them into scoring position. Getting on base and moving runners into scoring position is half of the offensive team's responsibility. The other half, hitting with men in scoring position and sustaining a rally, is discussed in detail in the next chapter. After men reach base, teams use several approaches to advance them into scoring position. Some teams use an aggressive approach by starting runners, using the hit-and-run, trying to stretch singles into doubles, going from first to third, and hitting behind runners. This type of offense relies on the premise that scoring a single run in any inning is a productive inning, which done often enough will achieve the main objective of scoring more runs than the opponent does.

Others subscribe to the style of getting runners on base but do not want to risk making outs on the bases. Therefore, they play a station-to-station type of offense. They prefer to wait for a multiple-hit inning or an extra-base hit to score runs. The high-scoring offense has the ability to do both: They can move runners into scoring position while avoiding the double play and score a single run, and they can collect a big inning at any moment during the game. Most teams seem to fall into one of two categories, either a small-ball team or a big-inning team. A high-scoring offense must have characteristics of both. Player personnel will determine, in large part, how teams approach getting players on base and getting them into scoring position. The amount of team speed and power, the balance of left- and right-handed hitting, and the proficiency with which they execute offensive skills determine the approach that the team will use.

RUN CREATION

A hitter's job is to contribute to run creation.

(Will, 1990)

How does a hitter help create runs? A hitter does that in one of the following four ways:

1. Getting on base
2. Getting runners to third base with less than two outs
3. Getting runners in from third base
4. Keeping the rally going

Some baseball purists measure a player's offensive contribution by his batting average.

It is a good measurement but is insufficient, for two reasons. First, not all hits are equal. Second, not all failures to hit are equal. Not all hits are equal, for two reasons. Some hits carry the hitter to more bases, closer to a run. And not all hits occur when they would be most productive, particularly when runners are in scoring position. (Will, 1990)

Getting on base and advancing runners into scoring position can be accomplished without a base hit.

SMALL BALL VERSUS BIG-INNING BALL

When I first started coaching, the philosophy that I was taught was "Get 'em on. Get 'em over. Get 'em in." The offense was predicated on having the leadoff man reach base and steal second. The next batter was to hit a ground ball to the right side, and another ground ball would score the runner from third. The offense would try to duplicate this model as many times as possible over the course of nine innings. At the conclusion of the game, if we executed this formula five times we felt good about our offensive execution. The problem, however, was that when our defense yielded a big inning and negated our one-run-per-inning tally, we would find ourselves on the short end of the win column too often against good teams.

After a decade of frustration we adopted the big-inning model. We played for a big inning early and would manufacture runs when necessary. The effect of freebies revolutionized how we approached the big inning. We realized that we did not need power to accomplish scoring three or more runs in an inning. Our goal was to score seven runs a game. We were able to achieve this goal consistently with the aid of the big inning but could not reach seven runs without one. I can only remember one game in my coaching career where we scored a single run in every inning of a game.

Playing for the big inning, defined as an inning of three or more runs, is a sound offensive approach given the fact that in 75% of all games the winning team scores more runs in one inning than the losing team scores in the entire game. Scoring the first run of the game has also proved to be advantageous statistically. The *1986 Elias Analyst* reported that scoring the first run gave the typical American League team, in 1985, a two-to-one edge on its opponents. In addition, the worst team in the league, after scoring first, had a better record than the best team in the league when its opponents scored first. An Elias study of the 1986 season showed that 65% of all American League games were won by the teams that scored that first run (Will, 1990).

The contrasting offensive philosophy is not to wait for the big inning but to take a run anytime you can get one, even if that means giving up an out to do so. The one-run-per-inning approach also subscribes to the tack-on approach, adding single runs as often as possible. According to Jim Lefebvre, "When we scored at least three different times in a game, our winning percentage was at least .600." There is, he says, a psychological advantage in getting the lead and then increasing it. That builds an expectation of defeat in the other team (Will, 1990).

Weaver Ball

Although teams can score runs in many ways, there are generally two schools of thought regarding how to go about scoring runs. The first is the Earl Weaver approach, or playing for the big inning.

> *Earl Weaver was a strong proponent of baseball's megatonnage. A manager's best friend, he said, is a three-run home run. He considered it irrational to bunt a runner over from second to third with no outs, counting on a sacrifice fly to drive him in. Weaver reasoned that a successful sacrifice bunt is by no means a lead pipe cinch, and that a sacrifice fly is harder to come by than people think. So leave the runner at second and hope for a single to bring him in rather than counting on two contingencies (the bunt, the sacrifice fly). (Will, 1990)*

This school of thought advocates playing for the big inning and not forcing the issue on the bases. In other words, do not risk making an out on the bases. They subscribe to the theory that an out on the bases is the worst out in baseball.

La Russa Approach

The other school of thought is the Tony La Russa approach: A single run is better than no run at all. This approach advocates "pushing," taking risks on the bases and forcing the defense to make plays under pressure.

> *"We wanted to establish an A's style of play," says La Russa, "A lot of effort and playing with an idea." La Russa's idea is to find a way to find an edge in every situation. As soon as some managers fall behind by even a run, they become less aggressive about starting runners or otherwise risking outs on a steal or hit-and-run. La Russa thinks such restraint is often unreasonable. (Will, 1990)*

They do not wait around for the home run. If a runner is at second base with no outs, the hitter is expected to hit a ground ball behind the runner and get him to third with less than two outs.

MOVING RUNNERS IN THE BBCOR ERA

The issue of getting on base and moving runners into scoring position has proved to be even more difficult with the institution of the new BBCOR bat in college baseball for 2011. Runs have been down almost a run and half per game, batting averages are down 25 points, and home runs are down almost 40% across the board. These bats have ushered in a new era in college baseball, a renewed emphasis on the short game and the importance of moving runners, and a pushing aside of the station-to-station era of the last two decades.

> *A station-to-station team, meaning a team that put runners on base and waits for the batter alone to make something happen, simply has fewer ways to score runs. You do not often string together three singles in an inning. True, if you take risks you can run yourself out of a big inning, and as La Russa says, "You don't want to shoot down your chance for a crooked number (more than one run)." But if you are aggressive in ways other than by blasting extra-base hits, you can put together big innings that are built in part out of the other team's anxieties. La Russa wants the other team to look out from its dugout "and get real bad vibes" about his team's physical and mental aggressiveness. (Will, 1990)*

Bat Control

Three primary bat-control skills are needed to move runners. The following skills must be mastered if an offense wants to score runs consistently:

1. Hit a hard ground ball to the right side of the infield on pitches in and out of the strike zone
2. Execute a hit-and-run, which requires the batter to hit a ground ball out of the middle of the field to avoid a double play
3. Execute a slash, which requires the hitter to pull the bat back and hit a ground ball in the 6 hole or 4 hole when the opponent is running the wheel play

On-Base Percentage

Every inning starts the same way, with no outs and nobody on base. The million-dollar question is, *How can the offense get the leadoff hitter on base?* The offense knows that if they can get the leadoff man on base at the start of an inning, they have a 95% chance of scoring. The defense, on the other hand, realizes that if they retire the leadoff batter, the offense has only a 30% chance of scoring that inning. The odds of scoring in an inning vary greatly based on the leadoff batter's ability to reach base. Getting on base is the launching point for the offense. Players who have a knack for getting on base are a valuable commodity. "The crucial concept in baseball is the creation of opportunities. That means putting people on base" (Will, 1990).

The phrase "a walk is as good as a hit" is true. The problem is that too many hitters do not see it that way. They are more concerned with their batting average and refuse to take a walk. They view a walk as an unproductive at-bat, a lost opportunity to collect a base hit. The mind-set of a productive offensive player should be to get on base any way that he can.

> *Walking is a part of a batter's duty. Steve Garvey . . . collected 2,599 hits and had six 200-hit seasons, but he would've been a more valuable asset to his team if he had walked more. He walked only once per 18.44 at-bats. Ted Williams averaged once per 3.82. "Stan Musial," says Earl Weaver, "was the best at adjusting once the ball left the pitcher's hand. He hit the pitcher's pitch. Williams was the best at making them throw his pitch. He did not believe in adjusting. That wasn't the pitch he wanted, he knew enough to walk to first base. That's why he hit .406." (Will, 1990)*

Ted Williams, arguably the greatest hitter who ever lived, believed that the two best stats in terms of evaluating the productivity of a hitter were on-base percentage and slugging percentage. If we combine these two statistics we have on-base percentage plus slugging percentage (OPS). We can hardly argue with Mr. Williams about these two important stats. A hitter with power can change the complexion of the game with one swing of the bat. A home run is the greatest offensive play in baseball because it is an instant run and cannot be defended. The walk is the second greatest offensive play because it cannot be defended either. Any other ball put in play that does not leave the ballpark can be defended and is a potential out.

Some baseball purists group hitters into two categories—those who score runs and those who drive them in. But players like Ted Williams can do both. On-base percentage is a measure of a player's ability to reach base. A hitter who can walk is a valuable commodity for the offense because he will most likely hit in the top half of the batting order to set the table for the run producers in the middle of the batting order.

LEADING OFF THE INNING

Every batter in the lineup has the opportunity to lead off an inning. One of the unique and fascinating elements of the game of baseball is that the leadoff batter in the lineup is guaranteed to lead off only in the first inning of the game. As a result, every batter in the lineup needs to have the skills to increase his odds of getting on base when he is the leadoff hitter. What are those skills?

Strike-Zone Awareness

The first skill is the batter's ability to swing at strikes and take balls. In his 1970 book *The Science of Hitting*, Ted Williams wrote that the strike zone

> *is approximately the width of seven baseballs, allowing for pitches on "the black" being called strikes. When a batter starts swinging at pitches just two inches out of that zone, he has increased the pitcher's target from approximate 4.2 square feet to about 5.8 square feet—an increase of 38%. Allow a pitcher that much of an advantage and you will be a .250 hitter. (Will, 1990)*

That point sounds elementary, but too many hitters swing at balls out of the strike zone and at pitches that are in the strike zone but are not good pitches to hit. Wade Boggs was quoted as saying, "My hitting zone is tighter than the strike zone." The hitter must realize that a strike is better than an out. Taking a strike is OK because if the hitter swings at a low, knee-high strike early in the count, the best he can do is hit a ground ball. If he were to take that pitch, however, it is only a strike, not an out. The pitcher has his greatest advantage over a hitter when the hitter is overanxious.

Hit-by-Pitch

The second weapon is the hitter's ability to hold his ground and get hit by a pitch. This issue is controversial in college baseball. The college rule states that a batter does not have to get out of the way of the ball, but he cannot intentionally try to get hit. When the ball is coming at them, some hitters become extremely jumpy, as if the ball had razor blades on it. Batters must learn the proper way to get hit by a pitch, primarily for safety, but also because reaching base by an HBP helps the team and is critical for a high-scoring offense. Pitchers are taught to throw inside, to move hitter's feet to let the hitter know that the plate belongs to the pitcher. The hitter must be taught how to protect himself and hold his ground in the batter's box.

This cat-and-mouse game between the hitter and pitcher determines dominance at the plate. The hitter must protect himself by turning his head, front shoulder, and front hip toward the backstop away from the pitcher, rolling to the inside and dropping the bat at the same time (figure 9.1). This action exposes the larger muscles in the upper back and protects the hands and face from injury. The hitter does not need to move his feet or snap his knees back away from the ball coming in. That reaction only helps the pitcher and reduces the batter's opportunity to reach first base safely on an extreme miss by the pitcher. The ability to take a pitch and avoid injury is a learned skill that must be worked on in practice. Players must be held accountable for holding their ground and turning away from the ball properly every day in practice and games.

Figure 9.1 Safely taking a pitch involves rolling to the inside and dropping the bat at the same time: *(a)* view from behind the plate; *(b)* view from the mound.

Bunt

The third weapon is the ability to bunt for a base hit. This weapon can be used against a pitcher who is really on that day or is a bad matchup for the hitter. His best opportunity to reach base might be to use a drag bunt or push bunt for a base hit. The threat of a bunt will also shorten up the corner infielders and decrease their lateral range, which could allow a weakly hit ball to find its way past one of the corner infielders.

Hit and Take

The last weapon is the hitter's ability to hit. This method is the most difficult way to reach base because the odds are against the hitter. A good strategy for the leadoff hitter of every inning is to go to the plate sitting on a fastball up in the zone on the outer half of the plate. If he gets that pitch he takes his best swing. If the first pitch is a ball the hitter must look down at the third-base coach, who may or may not give him the take sign for the next pitch. On a one ball, no strike count, the hitter's on-base percentage in major-league baseball goes up 10%. For example, if a hitter's on-base percentage is .300 before the first pitch is thrown in an 0-0 count, his on-base percentage jumps from .300 to .400 when the count goes to 1-0. If the batter gets the take sign, the offense is playing the odds trying to get one pitch closer to the all-important walk. The walk is the number two predictor of a big inning.

The take is unavoidable. Baseball is a team game, and winning is the goal. Hitters have to take pitches at times to improve the team's chances of winning. Several situations may warrant taking a pitch:

1. The leadoff hitter of an inning with a 1-0 count
2. Early in the game after the leadoff hitter in the inning is out on the first pitch
3. The hitter's first at-bat of the day so that he can get zeroed in on the pitcher's stuff and release point
4. The first pitch from a relief pitcher with poor control
5. Undisciplined hitters who are better hitters late in the count
6. Late in the game when the umpires tightens the strike zone
7. Early in the game when the team is down a lot of runs
8. After 16 pitches in an inning when pitchers tend to lose stuff and command

Practice Tip

During intrasquad games a good way to emphasize how important it is for the leadoff batter to reach base is to award the offense extra points if they get the leadoff man on. Another way to stress the importance of getting the leadoff batter on base is to move him from first to third base automatically. Although the defense will think that this modification is unfair, it highlights the fact that when the leadoff man reaches, the team will score 95% of the time.

RUNNER AT FIRST BASE

With a runner on first base and less than two outs, what is the next move for the offense? Do they let the batter swing away and tell the runner to react to a ball put in play, or do they force the action by starting the runner?

With no outs and a runner at first, taking a shot to right is a good play for three reasons. First, the first baseman is holding the runner, which leaves a big area, a canyon, between him and the second baseman. In addition, the second baseman has to cheat toward second to cover for the double play or possible steal, widening the hole even more. Second, hitting into a double play is less likely if the batter hits the ball to the second baseman's left. Third, on a hit to the right field the runner usually continues to third.

With one out the same points apply.

With two outs the offense is looking for an extra-base hit, but if the defense gives the batter the bunt, he should take it.

The greatest defensive play is a double play because the defense records two outs on one play. The double play has been called the pitcher's best friend because it has helped many a pitcher avoid a big inning. From an offensive standpoint, the double play is an instant rally killer that must be avoided.

> One of baseball's few recent dynasties, the Athletics of 1972 to 1974, won three consecutive world championships with a team batting average below that of the league over the three seasons. The Athletics did get a lot of long hits. And many of those long hits were preceded by walks. Furthermore, the Athletics had a high level of successful steals and (partly for that reason) a high rate of success at avoiding hitting into double plays. (Will, 1990)

An offense can employ several strategies to avoid the double play:

1. Straight steal
2. Hit-and-run or hit-and-run drive
3. Bunt
4. Dirt ball read

A high-powered offense must be able to use these weapons against a good defensive team that has an outstanding pitcher on the mound.

Practice Tip

Incorporate skills such as the hit-and-run, the hit-and-run drive, and the five bunts in batting practice regularly so that players feel comfortable and confident in executing those skills. In addition, practice those skills in the tunnel off a live arm.

Hit-and-Run

A hit-and-run is a good option to place a runner in scoring position and avoid the double play if two of the following three criteria are present: (1) a fast runner, (2) a pitcher who throws strikes, and (3) a batter who can put the ball in play. If two of those three criteria are in place, a hit-and-run might be the right call, especially if the pitcher is adept at shutting down the running game or if the catcher can really throw.

Hit-and-Run Drive

A hit-and-run drive is a unique play in which the offense starts the runner when the hitter is in an advantage count, most likely a 2-0 or 3-1, and is anticipating a fastball that he can drive into the gap. The runner is starting from first base and, if the play is executed perfectly, he will score if the ball is driven into the gap. In 1992 Pepperdine University scored the winning run in the national championship game of the College World Series on the hit-and-run drive.

Practice Tip

To simulate the hit-and-run and hit-and-run drive in batting practice, use base runners to provide the most gamelike scenario for the hitters. On a hit-and-run, the runner is running on the pitch, and the hitter's job is to hit the ball on the ground out of the middle of the infield (to avoid a double play). On a hit-and-run drive, the runner breaks on the pitch and the hitter, who is usually in a 2-0 or 3-1 count and anticipating a fastball, is trying to drive the ball into the gaps so that the runner can score from first.

READING THE BALL

One of the best indicators of an offensive team's focus and concentration is their ability to anticipate and break at the correct moment from first base, second base, or third base on a pitch in the dirt. An offense that does not miss moments like advancing on balls in the dirt, that does not have delayed reads in this situation, is an aggressive and finely tuned machine that is in attack mode. Dirt ball reads are free 90s. They can put runners into scoring position and help sustain rallies by eliminating the threat of the double play.

Dirt Ball Read

A simple drill is to have runners at every base, a pitcher on the mound, and a catcher in full gear. The runners at each base take their secondary leads and react to the pitch. If the catcher catches the ball, the runners take two hard steps back to their respective bases. If the ball is in the dirt, the runners advance to the next base but must follow these guidelines:

1. A runner at first reads the flight of the ball out of the pitcher's hand and runs before the ball hits the dirt.

2. A runner at second must see a lateral deflection off the catcher's chest protector to advance to third.

3. A runner at third becomes increasingly aggressive with every out. For example, with no outs the ball has to go to the backstop, but with two outs the ball may only have to trickle outside the 13-foot (4 m) dirt circle.

RUNNER AT SECOND BASE

What does "Get 'em over" mean? When a runner is at second base with no outs, the batter wants to advance the runner to third so that the next batter can drive him in without a base hit. Hitting behind the runner is a trademark of a proficient offense. In its purest sense, by hitting the ball behind the runner the offense trades an out for a run, but when a hitter does it aggressively he may produce an RBI single or at least put runners at first and third.

> *Not all "failures" are really failures. Some of them can contribute to run creation. The official score reflects this by not charging an at-bat when the hitter delivers a sacrifice or sacrifice fly. But a hitter who, with no outs and a runner on second, gives himself up by grounding to the right side of the infield, thereby enabling the runner to advance to third, has "failed" to get a hit but has succeeded at the team project of advancing the process of run creation. (Will, 1990)*

The over-and-in is not always an easy play to execute. The battle for supremacy at the plate in this situation is extremely heated because the pitcher will do everything he can to make the batter hit the ball to left side of the infield while the batter is doing everything he can to hit the ball to the right side of the infield (Will, 1990). In a perfect world for the offense, the ball would go in the four hole and the runner would score from second base. The batter would end up at second base when the outfielder tries to throw out the runner at home. Now the situation has replicated itself; the offense has a run in and another runner in scoring position. The fallback plan would be for the batter to hit a hard ground ball to the right side of the infield, at the very least advancing the runner to third.

A right-handed hitter must be able to hit a hard ground ball to the right side of the infield to advance a runner from second to third. The pitcher will make it difficult on the right-handed batter to do so by busting him inside with fastballs or by throwing him slow pitches down in the zone, making it difficult for him to carve the ball to the right side.

The left-handed hitter has the advantage of being able to pull the ball to the right side of the infield, which for many hitters is an easier skill than hitting the ball on the ground to the back side of the field. The pitcher will try to induce a left-handed hitter to hit the ball to left side of the infield by throwing him balls on the outer half the plate. This game within the game, the confrontation between the pitcher and the hitter, is the essence of baseball. The hitter must win this battle if the offense is to score runs consistently.

With no outs, trying to hit behind the runner is considered smart baseball. A hitter is trying to get the man over by going the other way, but he should try to accomplish this aggressively. The philosophy here is to advance the runner with a hit but to settle for the ground ball out. The other options here for right-hander would be a push bunt to the right side. A lefty can "take it with him" to produce similar positive results.

With one out, the hitter's job is to hit the ball hard, anywhere. He can figure his quality at-bat average and count his RBIs.

With two outs, his job is easy! He just needs to buckle down and concentrate on hitting a line drive down, through the middle.

How does a right-handed batter go about hitting the ball the other way?

1. Get a pitch out over the plate.
2. The hands and wrists lead the bat through the hitting zone. The barrel trails the hands, and the right elbow stays in close to the body.
3. Never let the barrel of the bat fall below the level of your hands.
4. Allow the ball to travel deeper into the strike zone. Try to make contact with the ball while it is over home plate. Do this by waiting longer as the ball travels toward you before starting your swing. By waiting longer you have less chance of being fooled by something off-speed and pulling off the ball.
5. Try to hit the inner half of the ball, the part of the ball closest to you. Doing this will help you concentrate and stay on the ball longer, especially when chasing those nasty breaking balls. This approach is called inside-out hitting.

A simple, straightforward way of training a hitter to hit the other way is to use the extreme inside-out tee method (figure 9.2). Line up the tee with the hitter's belly button and have him stand 18 inches (45 cm) from the ball. Place the ball on the tee with a vertical two-seam fastball alignment. The hitter should stare at the inside seam and drive his hands inside the ball, hitting the ball on the barrel of the bat and driving it to the opposite corner of the tunnel. This method reinforces the concept of keeping the bat shaft tight to the shoulder and the hands inside the ball. The hitter learns kinesthetically how to bring his hands inside the flight of the ball.

Figure 9.2 Extreme inside-out tee drill forces the batter to keep shaft-to-shoulder in order to hit the ball off the barrel.

Get 'Em Over, Get 'Em In

Equipment

Pitching machine set on a fastball speed appropriate to the players' skill level.

Setup

The drill takes place on the game field; the pitching machine is set in front of the mound.

Execution

With 16 hitters, start with 8 players at second base and 8 players at home. Each hitter has a partner who is a base runner. After the hitter puts the ball in play, the batter–runner and base runner react accordingly and then switch roles.

Round 1: The hitter's job is to hit a ground ball to the right side of the infield, thereby advancing the runner from second base with no outs ("Get 'em over"). All 16 players take a turn as hitter and base runner.

Round 2: Begin with the runner at third base. Repeat the process.

Coaching points

Base runners need to run with their eyes up. Also, if the batted ball hits the L-frame, the runner should not advance because the frame simulates the pitcher.

Variations

When runners reach third base, the infield may stay back, so the hitter's job is to hit a ground ball to either the second baseman or the shortstop to "get 'em in" from third. The infield can also play in with a runner at third. Now the hitter's job is to hit a fly ball to the outfield to score the runner.

Common errors and corrections

The biggest problem that right-handed hitters have in this drill is hitting around the ball, which prevents them from hitting it to the back side of the field and advancing the runner. Because they are hitting off a machine that is throwing a lot of strikes, the drill provides a lot of repetition, promoting self-correction and mastery.

CHAPTER 10

RBI Situations

*There is no greater pleasure in the world than walking up to the plate
with men on base and knowing that you are feared.*

Ted Simmons, former major-league catcher and switch hitter

In the previous chapter, we discussed the first two offensive plays, getting on base and moving runners into scoring position. This chapter discusses the last two offensive plays, hitting with runners in scoring position and sustaining rallies. We will focus on a detailed plan for success when hitting in these two situations, which includes physical adjustments, a mental approach, and ways to attack various types of pitchers.

The old adage "RBIs live through the middle back side of the field" has proved to be true. Pitchers tend to bear down with runners in scoring position. They focus more intensely and are less apt to give in, to lay fastballs over the middle of the plate, because they may be willing to concede a walk in an RBI situation. Batters can expect to see a plethora of off-speed pitches and fringe fastballs, those that are around the plate and are meant for effect and not designed to be strikes. Pitchers also expand the strike zone in RBI situations to exploit a hitter's tendency to be overanxious because he wants to be the hero. As major-league legend Pete Rose said, "A hitter's impatience is the pitcher's biggest advantage."

The hitter who wants to be productive in RBI situations must not chase pitches outside the strike zone and must be willing to hit the ball through the middle back side of the field. The hitter who reacts to the pitcher can take only what he is given. Hall of Famer Mike Schmidt offered this advice:

> You must stay geared up the middle on the ground. You can't think about pulling the ball with men in scoring position because, most of the time, a pitcher will try to trick the hitter there or throw him off stride by throwing a breaking ball. The guys who go for the home runs and try to go for too much too early in the count become easy outs. That was my problem the first five or six years of my career.

THREE CARDINAL SINS IN RBI SITUATIONS

Hitters make three big mistakes with runners in scoring position:

1. Sitting fastball on every pitch
2. Trying to pull the ball
3. Chasing pitches outside the strike zone

Pitchers exploit these three tendencies. It gets back to the question from chapter 6: Who is in control of the at-bat, the pitcher or the hitter? Hitters who understand that drawing a walk in an RBI situation is a quality at-bat and that it contributes to a potential big inning are less apt to try to do too much at the plate. This skill is important when hitting with men in scoring position. As Mike Schmidt said, "Do less, not more, with runners in scoring position."

Pitchers attack hitters differently in RBI situations, and hitters must be able make the adjustment. A hitter might observe his teammates come to the plate with runners in scoring position before he faces the pitcher that day, so by observation he can start to figure out the pitcher's pitch patterns and sequences with runners in scoring position. According to Frank Robinson,

> *The two most important fundamentals a hitter should know if he hopes to reach the majors and stay there are to learn as much as possible about the pitcher, and be aware of the game situation when going to the plate.*

What pitch does he like to start hitters off with when runners are in scoring position? Steve Springer said that with runners in scoring position the first pitch is an off-speed pitch 80% of the time. The hitter who goes to the plate looking for a fastball on the first pitch with guys in scoring position will be wrong 80% of the time. Hitters must watch and focus on the patterns of the pitcher so that they are prepared when they get in the box. Hitters must also be keenly aware of the pitcher's put-away pitch, the pitch that he likes to throw with two strikes. This knowledge is vital because often all the hitter needs to do is put the ball in play to cash in the RBI.

We will delve into the five main RBI situations that a batter will face during a game: (1) second or third base, two outs; (2) third base, no outs; (3) third base, one out; (4) first and third, less than two outs; and (5) bases loaded, less than two outs. A productive offensive player must be able to execute in these five RBI situations. Any team that hopes to put a lot of runs on the scoreboard must be proficient at driving in runners when they are in scoring position. Many coaches and players have been frustrated at the conclusion of a ballgame when they look at the box score and see that their team has left 10 or more runners in scoring position. The difference between victory and defeat is often as slim as one run. A losing team can frequently point to numerous failed attempts to cash in on RBI opportunities throughout the game. "If we could have just put the ball in play in that situation, we could have won the ballgame," coaches frequently say.

One of the keys to hitting with men in scoring position is to have what we call an approach, a mental and physical strategy for success. For every RBI situation we have a buzz phrase that defines for the hitter the outcome that we want to produce (see table 10.1). It clarifies his mental and physical approach at the plate in that particular situation. The buzz phrase "two-out RBI" means a line drive down. When the hitter hears "two-out RBI," he immediately knows that he is expected to hit a hard ground ball back through the middle of the field.

Connecting a specific approach to a specific situation is a valuable tool because a coach can grade the player's intent. For example, during intrasquad games when there are two outs and runners in scoring position, the expectation for the batter is to hit the ball hard on the ground through the middle of the diamond and force the defense to make a play. The coach sees the hitter swing straight up and pop up the ball, which is the opposite of the approach he wants. He knows that the player has the wrong approach, both physically and mentally. The coach can then make the necessary adjustments because

Table 10.1 Situational Approach Buzz Words

Situation	Buzz word	Approach
2 outs	"2 out RBI"	Line drive off pitcher's knees Never make the last out of the inning in the air
3rd base, infield back	"Play pepper"	GB up the middle Swing early in the count The RBI is more important than a base hit
3rd base, infield in	"Automatic"	Stay inside the ball Get a ball up in the zone
1st and 3rd	"Grand cannon" or "Automatic"	Lefties hit the 4-hole Righties stay inside the ball No rollovers to the pull side Most DPs are initiated on the left side of the infield
Bases loaded	"Knockout punch"	Drive the ball in the opposite field gap, clearing the bases and delivering the "knockout punch." Keep the ball off the ground. A strikeout is better than an inning-ending DP.

an expectation and detailed game plan was in place regarding what to do when runners are in scoring position with two outs.

In a typical nine-inning ballgame, an offense accumulates approximately 40 at-bats. A simple breakdown tells us that of those 40 at-bats, 9 will be to lead off an inning, which is approximately 25% of the at-bats during the game. Approximately another 10 at-bats will occur with runners in scoring position, accounting for another 25% of all plate appearances. The remaining 20 at-bats, or 50% percent, are free at-bats, at-bats when no runners are in scoring position and when the hitter is not leading off the inning. But during those 20 at-bats a player may be asked to move a runner; his primary job may not be trying to get a base hit. Of the 40 at-bats, a hitter will have two strikes on him 50% of the time. These numbers help us understand the frequency with which events take place throughout a typical game, which in turn helps the coach and player understand workloads during practice.

To become proficient at any skill, an athlete must have realistic, quality repetitions that simulate game situations. The previous information suggests that hitters should spend a minimum of 25% of their time on hitting with runners in scoring position and 50% of their time working on two-strike hitting. Buzz phrases are quick reminders of the correct approach that a hitter should have in a given RBI situation. These mental strategy reminders are helpful in competition because they are short, to the point, and memorable.

GET 'EM IN

The next three sections cover situations with runners in scoring position. "Get 'Em In" refers to the batter's ability to collect an RBI in these situations.

"Two-Out RBI": Two Outs, Runner in Scoring Position

We have all heard the saying "Two-out RBIs win ballgames." This situation arises numerous times during a contest. The difficult thing about executing in this situation is that the hitter must get a base hit to drive in the run. We are back to a player's batting average, which for most hovers around the .300 mark. This statistic means that the hitter is going to fail in this situation 70% of the time. We want to provide the hitter with a different mind-set, one that doesn't require him to get a base hit so that he believes that he has a better than 30% chance at being successful. We want the hitter to have the mind-set of having a quality at-bat instead of thinking about getting a base hit. With two outs, the hitter can be productive in several ways without collecting a base hit. For example, a walk, hit-by-pitch, well-placed bunt, or well-struck ball all create pressure on the defense and cause anxiety, which can result in defensive mistakes, thereby increasing the odds of success. In essence, the hitter always has one goal: to achieve a quality at-bat.

The worst thing that can happen in this situation is for the hitter to hit a routine fly ball or pop-up that the defense can easily catch to record the last out of the inning. We have a saying, "You never want the defense to run off the field after a pop-up or strikeout looking." We do not want to give the defense this possible momentum shifter. With two outs and a runner in scoring position, the defense is aware that any mistake on their part could lead to a run. The offense must take advantage of this anxiety and do everything it can to put the ball in play, especially on a line or on the ground, to force the defense to field and throw the ball to record an out.

To reinforce to hitters the concept of line drive down, in batting practice the hitters should focus on hitting balls off the L-frame when practicing two-out RBI situations. Mike Schmidt, Hall of Fame third baseman of the Philadelphia Phillies, used this approach exclusively when he was at the plate. His last thought before swinging was to hit a line drive off the pitcher's knees. With two outs and runners in scoring position, the hitter should try to hit a line drive down through the middle of the field. This approach capitalizes on the anxiety of the defense, which could lead to a run by forcing the defense to field and throw a ball to record an out.

Practice Tip

In batting practice, the coach calls out the buzz phrase "two-out RBI," and the hitter responds by attempting to hit the ball hard off the L-frame. The L-frame gives the hitter a target to shoot at and immediate feedback.

"Play Pepper": Runner at Third, Infield Back, Less Than Two Outs

With a runner at third, less than two outs, and the infield playing back, the hitter is in a great position to collect an RBI because he can do so without getting a base hit. To be in this position, the hitter has benefited from his teammate's ability not only to get on base but also to propel himself around the bases. The hitter needs only to put the ball in play on the ground in the middle of the field for the runner to score. This situation is a prime example of team baseball; each hitter who contributed passed the baton to the next to make a successful chain that manufactures the run. In this situation, the offense needs an unselfish at-bat, a hitter who understands that an RBI is more important than a base hit.

The buzz phrase here is "play pepper," which means that the batter is to get on top of the baseball and hit it through the middle of the field. Less-skilled hitters might consider making their two-strike adjustments from the first pitch by spreading out, getting closer to the plate, choking up on the bat, and shortening their stroke. All of this helps ensure ground-ball contact, which increases the odds of getting the runner in from third base with the infield back.

Another important buzz phrase that is applicable in this situation is "Brooks Robinson." We say this to hitters in this situation to conjure up the image of a great defender at third base who, if the ball is hit to him, will simply field the ball, throw home, and eliminate the RBI. With a runner at third base, the infield back, and less than two outs, a right-handed hitter must not hook the ball to third base. Pitchers will try to entice a right-handed hitter to hook the baseball by busting him inside with fastballs or getting him way out front with an off-speed pitch down in the zone. This tactic by the pitcher is one of the few ways to prevent the offense from scoring the runner from third with the infield back. Certainly, a strikeout, a ball hit back to the pitcher, or a shallow fly ball will also nullify the RBI opportunity in this situation. These at-bats can be frustrating for the offense because the defense is essentially conceding one run in the hope of staying out of the big inning. The hitter must do three things correctly with his bat path to ensure that he hits a firm ground ball through the middle of the diamond:

1. Maintain the shaft to the shoulder (use an inside-out stroke) (figure 10.1).
2. Keep the barrel above the flight of the ball until contact (figure 10.2).
3. Extend through contact (keep the barrel flat through contact and finish) (figure 10.3).

Another key in RBI situations is for the hitter to keep his front side down and in. To use the middle back side of the field, the hitter must close down at release. This skill is critical, especially in RBI situations, because the pitcher is going to throw more off-speed pitches in hopes that the hitter will pull off the ball and hit around the baseball, producing a weak big-hop ground ball.

Figure 10.1 Shaft to shoulder.

Figure 10.2 Barrel above the flight of the ball.

Figure 10.3 Extension through contact.

The last key for the batter in this situation is what we like to call early action, which means that the hitter tries to put the ball in play early in the count. Because a strikeout is the worst outcome in this situation, the goal of early action is to avoid hitting with two strikes with a runner in scoring position. Although using this approach may cause some hitters to swing at borderline pitches, this is not necessarily detrimental because the hitter does not have to get a base hit; he just needs to make contact on the ground. Hence, his pitch selection does not have to be as fine to achieve a quality at-bat and collect an RBI.

> **Practice Tip**
>
> In standard batting practice format, put base runners on third base and practice hitting with no outs and the infield back and with one out and the infield back on a daily basis. Place a screen halfway down the third-base line to protect the runner. The BP pitcher should change speeds on the hitter to simulate a game situation. Coaches can evaluate the players' intent; they should be on top of the baseball, up the middle, and on the ground, which is the essence of playing pepper.

No Outs If the infield is back and conceding the run, a simple ground ball may do the trick. But a right-handed hitter has to realize that he cannot score the run if he hits the ball to the third baseman or pitcher. Hitting here is simple because all the pressure is on the pitcher to make perfect pitches. The hitter should look for the ball over the plate and up in the strike zone so that he can drive the ball.

One Out The only thing that varies in this situation as opposed to no outs is that the hitter should be more aware of hitting up the middle or the other way. With no outs, the hitter has the freedom to be aggressive with the bat. With one out, he has to get the run home. Pulling off the ball here is a no-no. By thinking "middle of the diamond," the batter can wait longer and track the ball deeper in the zone, allowing for better contact.

"Automatic": Runner at Third and Infield In

When a runner is at third with less than two outs, the defense is in a desperate situation when they elect to play the infield in. The offense is in a great position to push across a run, extend the inning, and continue to apply pressure. The decreased range of the infielders because of their proximity to the hitter creates more holes for the hitter to deliver an RBI. The buzzword here is "automatic," which means that the hitter must attack the inside part of the baseball. This approach helps ensure that the hitter will not pull off the ball and hit the outside part of the baseball, which often produces a weakly hit big-hop ground ball. Big-hop grounders are easier for the infielders to get to because they are pounded into the ground, so the fielders have more time to react.

The other benefit of driving the inside part of the baseball, especially when pitches are elevated, is that they produce line drives and fly balls, either of which can produce an RBI. The hitter should focus on attacking the inside part of the baseball, but he should also be looking for a pitch up in the zone. This is no different from the standard approach to hitting:

1. Sitting on what you are going to get

2. Looking for a pitch up in the strike zone

3. Attacking the inside part of the baseball

This approach to hitting works no matter what the situation is. All-Star first baseman Albert Pujols has said that staying inside the baseball is a product of a good swing.

If the infield is in late in the game, the hitter must make sure that he gets a good pitch to hit, preferably one that is out over the plate and up in the strike zone to produce the needed fly ball. The hitter should remain aggressive in this situation, remembering that the pressure is on the pitcher. Being an early count hitter is best in this situation.

Practice Tip

The hitter must be sure that his front shoulder is pointed directly at the pitcher. This alignment will prevent him from pulling his head out of position and help him follow the ball. Keeping the front shoulder down and in is one of the keys for driving the ball up the middle. Pointing the front shoulder at the pitcher gives the hitter a better chance of hitting the ball where he is aiming, up the middle (UTM).

KEEP THE RALLY GOING (STAY OUT OF THE DOUBLE PLAY)

Learning how to sustain rallies is an important element for the high-scoring offense. It is often the difference between scoring one or two runs and getting that all-important big inning.

"Automatic": Runners at First and Third With Less Than Two Outs

With runners at first and third and no outs, the inning has the potential to develop into a big inning, characterized by scoring three or more runs. The buzzword for the proper mental and physical strategy for a right-handed hitter in this situation is "automatic." The hitter's intent should be to drive the ball to the right-center-field gap. Doing so may score both runners, and the hitter would find himself in scoring position with no outs. If he were to hit a deep fly ball into the RCF gap, both runners would be able to tag. One runner would score, and the other runner would end up at second.

The other option for a right-handed hitter is to hit a ground ball to the second baseman's glove side in the four hole, forcing him to throw to first. The offensive team would have a run across the board and another runner in scoring position. Quality at-bats like these are the result when the hitter executes the correct approach.

The right-handed hitter wants to avoid hitting the outside part of the baseball, which often results in a ground ball to left side of the infield that can result in a double play. A left-handed hitter, on the other hand, has the advantage of being able to pull the ball into the expanded four hole because the first baseman is holding the runner. The buzz phrase here for a left-handed hitter is "Grand Canyon," which alerts the hitter that a huge hole is open on the right side of the infield through which he should drive the ball. The left-handed hitter can strike the outside part of the baseball in this situation to drive the ball past the first baseman, which will get the run in, avoid the double play, and may allow the runner on first to go to third base.

No Outs   The batter should use the right side. A push bunt is also a great play because it can score a run and advance another runner into scoring position. The batter might even beat it out for a hit. The offense is still in a fly-ball situation for a run. The hitter should look for the ball up and over the plate, something to drive. He should be aggressive early in the count and avoid getting buried deep in the count. Hitting with a 2-1 count is easier than hitting 1-2.

One Out   The goal here is to get the run home. The hitter should take a shot at the right side or a hit a deep fly ball. The best approach is to hit early in the count when the pressure is on the pitcher.

"Knockout Punch": Bases Loaded Less Than Two Outs

With the bases loaded and less than two outs, the offense is looking to score three or more runs. In this situation, if the defense holds the offense to two runs or less, it has won the skirmish and may gain some momentum from a small moral victory. The buzz phrase for the hitter is "knockout punch," which conveys to the hitter that he is to drive the ball into the opposite-field gap. If the hitter is able to do this, he will clear the bases and will have delivered the knockout punch. With one swing of the bat, the game might be over.

At all costs, the batter must keep the ball off the ground in a bases-loaded situation. The risk of a double play is too great on any ground ball. In batting practice when the hitter hears the phrase "bases-loaded drill," he understands that for that round he must stay inside the baseball and keep the ball off the ground. Calling out the buzz phrases in batting practice and setting up the various situations is an effective way to get batters comfortable with executing each skill. Using daily intrasquad games to focus on the various situations and buzz phrases allows every batter to experience each situation and learn to execute the proper mental and physical strategy for success. By resetting the situation after each batter, the coach can grade the intent of each player.

At the conclusion of the intrasquad game, the coach can provide feedback to all the hitters about the situations that they encountered that day and remind them of the proper approach. For example, the situations covered that day in an intrasquad game might be runners at first and third and bases loaded. In both situations, the buzzword is "automatic," meaning that the hitter is to attack the inside part of the baseball and keep the ball off the ground. If the defense was unable to turn any double plays during the intrasquad game, the offense was at least moderately successful.

Other examples would be a runner at third with the infield back and a runner at second with no outs. In both situations a ground ball to the right side of the infield will advance the runner and produce a quality at-bat. If no fly balls were hit that day during the intrasquad game, the hitters' intent was excellent. They were trying to get on top of the baseball and hit ground balls to advance the runners. These examples show ways of training hitters to use the proper mental and physical approach in RBI situations. This method allows the coach to provide players with feedback while simplifying the five RBI situations.

No Outs   The objective here is to keep the rally going, drive in runners, and stay out of the double play. Again, the batter should get a pitch up and out over the plate that he can drive deep into the outfield gaps. The pressure is all on the pitcher. He has to throw strikes and come after the batter. The hitter must be ready and drive the ball to the opposite gap.

One Out   As with no outs, the batter wants to hit early and hit hard, preferably in the air to the opposite gap. A strikeout in this situation is better than a ground-ball double play. At least with a strikeout, the inning is still alive and the baton passes to the next batter.

PROPER MIND-SET

A big part of hitting is the player's mind-set. How he thinks of himself as a hitter, as well as how he deals with success and failure at the plate, will determine how good he will ever be as a hitter, regardless of his skill level.

Hitters have to make every day, every single at-bat, a new day. They must deal with the present and realize that they have no control over the past. Hitters must not place too much weight on their shoulders by trying to make up for things that happened yesterday. A hitter has no control over certain things. If he believes that he has to get three hits in a game, he is thinking incorrectly. The batter has no control over how many hits he is going to get on a particular day. After the batter hits the ball, everything is out of his hands.

But a hitter does have control over the following:

1. Timing
2. Work habits
3. Mental approach
4. Aggressiveness at the plate
5. Pitch selection

When batters do all that they can to control these factors and concentrate on having quality at-bats, the hits will take care of themselves. If a hitter can do these things, he might have the mind-set of the great Hall of Famer Rogers Hornsby who said, "I don't like to sound egotistical, but every time I step up to the plate with a bat in my hands, I feel sorry for the pitcher."

PART III

Competitive Preparation

More important than setting the goals is the follow-up—attention to detail, demand for practice perfection, and all the things that separate the teams that win from those that don't. All good performance starts with clear goals, but it's the day-to-day process of observing and monitoring your team's performance that makes the critical difference in the end.

Ken Blanchard and Don Shula, The Little Book of Coaching

Designed practices that enhance a team's offensive productivity and monitor player performance are critical to producing a high-powered offense. Incorporating the six elements of offense daily, through proper drills and competitive games improves, player skill development. Game-day preparation can be enhanced through a proper warm-up, consisting of a detailed batting practice routine and baserunning scheme. Focusing on the four offensive goals places the attention on the game instead of the opponent. The evaluation process, utilizing grade cards and grading periods, helps keep the high-scoring offense on track through the course of a long season.

CHAPTER 11

Organizing Effective Practices

Teams earn the opportunity to win based on the quality of their practices.

Ed Cheff, former head baseball coach, Lewis–Clark State College

To organize effective practices, the coach needs to consider the big picture first and cover all the components of offense in the fall and early spring. An offensive checklist, a detailed calendar, and an organized practice schedule will help the coach cover the components of a high-scoring offense thoroughly. This level of detail will also assist the coach in tracking how many times he covers each area within the given week and throughout the fall and spring season. Coaches need to spend their time wisely and devote the bulk of their time to what is most important. You can find a sample team practice schedule, an offensive checklist, and a sample practice plan at the end of the chapter; blank templates of some of the plans and checklists can also be found at www.humankinetics.com/hkmedialibrary/hk_media_library/high-scoring-baseball-tables.

When designing practices on the offensive side of the ball, the six elements of offense can serve as the road map in terms of planning.

No offense can score a lot of runs if it is proficient in only one of the six areas. An offense that is consistently scoring seven or more runs is firing on all cylinders. These six elements, used collectively, can overwhelm a defense. The goal is to incorporate these six areas in practice every day so that the offense gets the proper number of quality repetitions. Within these six elements of offense is the cornerstone of a high-scoring offense—the eight ways to achieve a quality at-bat. Listed here is an outline of the six elements of offense. This model should be used to construct practice on a daily, weekly, and seasonal basis.

1. Hitting
   a. 3-8 (hard ball contact)
   b. Less than two strikes and two strikes
   c. RBI situations
2. Bat control
   a. Over and in
   b. Hit-and-run
   c. Slash
3. Baserunning
   a. One base
   b. Two bases
4. Base stealing
   a. Second
   b. Third
   c. Home
   d. Double steal

5. Bunting

   a. Sacrifice—first base, third base

   b. Drag

   c. Push

   d. Safety squeeze and squeeze

   e. Slash

6. Strike-zone discipline

   a. Walk

   b. HBP

   c. Eight-pitch at-bat

Practices should prepare players to execute the coach's philosophy in games. Drills should enhance biomechanical development, train the mental approach, and refine timing in a controlled environment, and players must be challenged through a series of competitive drills to learn to execute under pressure. Coaches should follow a progression like the one described in the next section.

PRACTICE PROGRESSION

To train hitters, repetition needs to occur in a controlled environment. A progression of drills should culminate with training hitters above real time. These drills become more advanced in terms of difficulty, execution, and pressure.

1. Cage drills, tee drills (scripted progression for biomechanical development)

2. Ball-in-flight drills, front toss (timing and approach)

3. Six-station BP

4. Two pitch/coach–pitch scrimmage

5. Integrated Offensive Components (IOC: batting practice where the batters start with a 1-1 count, runners are paired up with the hitters in nine different situations)

   a. Base runners

   b. Batter starts with a 1-1 count

   c. Nine situations

6. Modified intrasquads

   a. Theme: Every intrasquad has a defined purpose.

   b. Approach: Grade intent; every hitter faces same situation.

   c. Situations: Reset after each batter.

    d. Counts: 0-0, 1-1, 1-2

    e. Base running: Steal within three pitches, mandatory two-base advancement.

    f. Compete: Keep points and monitor pace of game.

    g. Coaches: Coach third and call pitches.

7. Two-strike hitting versus a pitcher with a runner on third base and less than two outs

    a. Two teams compete against each other for points

8. Small game (bunter starts with two strikes)

    a. Two teams compete against each other for points

Ten Commandments of Practice

To help ensure that practices will be efficient and productive, the coach must help players understand expectations in terms of attitude, effort, and performance. The following example of practice guidelines defines expectations in these terms.

1. Report on time and in proper uniform (hat on correctly, sleeves not rolled up, shirttails tucked in, and so on).
2. Players must be fully dressed before entering the field.
3. Check the practice schedule upon arriving at the field.
4. Know your responsibilities and daily assignments.
5. Know the quote of the day.
6. All movement on the field is on the run.
7. Baserunning is done at full speed.
8. When group activity is stopped, everyone gives attention.
9. During on-field meetings everyone takes a knee.
10. Practices will be characterized by a high level of intensity and game-level enthusiasm. The coaching staff will not tolerate a lack of hustle. An offending player gets one warning. On the second occurrence, the player will be dismissed from practice (Ed Cheff, Lewis–Clark State College).

CAGE DRILLS (INSIDE)

The purpose of hitting drills is not only to improve a hitter from a biomechanical standpoint but also to enhance his timing and approach. A good hitting drill exposes a hitter's weakness and encourages him to make the necessary adjustments. We use a series of progressive drills that are challenging and emphasize the critical elements in hitting. Our hitting drills emphasize six key factors:

Elements in Hitting	Verbal Cues
1. Vision and timing	"See it longer, see it less."
	"Let the ball travel its proper distance."
2. Bat path and hand action	"Forward down to level, level."
	"Hand pivot back to belly button."
3. Weight shift and balance	"Knee to knee."
	"Start to finish."
4a. Approach with less than two strikes	"Sit on what you are going to get up in the zone and attack the inside part of the ball."
4b. Approach with two strikes	"Late and on top."
5. Adjustments	Pitch to pitch.
	Ask LOUE: late, over, under, early.
6. Outcome	"3-8 and you will be great."
	Eight ways to get a quality at-bat.

Players practice these six factors as they develop the correct swing through a number of mandatory repetitions. The repetitions should include the following:

1. Using medicine balls (bounce a 10-pound ball with the bottom hand under and the top hand fingers up from the hitting position to a partner 30 feet away; repeat 10 times)
2. Hitting a punching bag
3. Bat throws (fungos in a straight line)
4. Tee drills
   a. High
   b. Mid
   c. Low
5. Self-toss

6. Side toss
7. Front toss
   a. Two-step walk-up (20 feet [6.1 m])
   b. Angle (20 degrees)
   c. Behind

BALL-IN-FLIGHT DRILLS

After the ball is put in flight hitters have difficulty producing a biomechanically sound swing, arriving on time, and executing in various situations. The purpose of each drill is to expose a weakness and allow the hitter to make an immediate adjustment. Hitters who can perform proper hitting skills when the ball is in flight are ready for the final test, a real game.

Machine

Slow curveballs

Curveballs in RBI situations

Fastball velocity (90 mph [145 km/h]) from 60 feet, 6 inches (18.4 m); 57 feet, 6 inches (17.5 m); 54 feet, 6 inches (16.6 m)

For example, hitting a slow 12-6 breaking ball from 60 feet, 6 inches (18.4 m) forces the hitter to wait on the baseball to travel its proper distance before striking it. In most situations the break on the curveball does not make the hitter miss; the speed is what makes the hitter mis-hit the ball. The margin of error when hitting the curveball is the bottom inside half of the baseball. We want the hitter to avoid circling the baseball, because hitting the outside half creates a big-hop ground ball that can become a double play. In simplistic terms, if the batter is under the curveball he's on it; if he's over the curveball he's not.

Practicing against a machine that is throwing fastballs in the upper 80s to low 90s (140 to 148 km/h) forces the hitter to get on top of the ball and learn to adjust his timing. This practice also lets the hitter work on his approach. The approach on the fastball is different from the approach on the curveball. The approach to the fastball is to square it up, and the margin of error is the top of the baseball rather than the bottom of the baseball.

Because the rate of failure is high in hitting, challenging drills can make hitters feel as if all they do is fail. Although hitters should have the goal of hitting line drives, they also need to learn the right way to fail. Failing forward is critical in their development and pursuit of being productive offensive players. We use a saying "two-of-three," which reminds hitters that there is a right way to execute a skill and a right way to fail. We simply want to stay away from failing in the wrong way. Everyone is going to fail, but those who fail the right way will eventually execute properly more often than others.

For example, when hitting a curveball the goal is to arrive on time and strike the ball squarely on the barrel with backspin. The hitter who is attacking the inside part of the curveball will not always hit the ball squarely but may instead hit too much of the bottom of the baseball. In this instance the hitter mis-hits the ball, possibly resulting in a fly ball, but he is on the right track. The margin of error when hitting the curveball is the bottom inside of the ball, and that is the right way to fail. For us, that margin of error is acceptable because this hitter is close to executing properly. The hitter who circles the ball, striking the outside top of the baseball, is the hitter who has failed the wrong way. This kind of failure often produces the big-hop double-play ground ball that will get you beat.

When practicing against velocity, the hitter is expected to hit the ball hard with backspin on the barrel. If he hits the top of the baseball and hits the ball on the ground, he is on the right track; he has failed correctly. If, however, he is underneath the flight of a good fastball and pops the ball up, he has failed in the wrong way. A hitter who cannot catch up to above-average velocity pitches typically will be under the fastball. This hitter must focus on the top of the baseball against a pitcher with an above-average fastball.

Three types of batting practice

1. Offset (BP pitcher throws from seven steps from the rubber to the third-base line and the first-base line in alternating rounds)
   a. Purpose: to teach the proper contact point, which should produce a line drive right back over the BP pitcher's head
   b. Best swing (all swings with less than two strikes)
   c. Hitters should never overspin balls to the pullside
   d. Hitters should never be under (routine fly balls) to the back side of the field.
2. Game (throw-down base and strike zone)
   a. Purpose: to prepare hitters to execute the skills that they will need in a game
   b. Round 1: graduate power ground balls off the grass to the back side of the field (fastball); drag
   c. Round 2: up the middle, fast and slow pitches; push
   d. Round 3: cripple count (3-1 fastball); sacrifice, first base side bunt
   e. Round 4: RBI (fastball and curveball); safety squeeze bunt
   f. Round 5: two strikes (mix pitches); slash

3. Dual BP (at home plate)

    a. Purpose: to maximize repetitions by dividing hitters into two turtles (portable batting cages; see figure 11.1)

    b. 50% with less than two strikes

    c. 50% with two strikes

We like to use three types of batting practice formats, each with a defined purpose. The first is offset hitting. We set up two L-frames, one on the second-base side of the mound and one on the shortstop side of the mound, each seven steps toward their respective bases. The hitters complete one round facing the pitcher on the second-base side and then an entire round on the shortstop side. The hitters are working on taking their best swings and back spinning the ball over the L-frame where the pitcher is located. This drill helps reinforce the mentality that we want from our hitters with less than two strikes—to hit hard backspin line drives off the sweet spot of the bat. A good teaching point is to remind hitters never to be over on the pull side (big-hop ground ball) or under to the back side (routine fly ball). These results are the wrong way to fail.

Figure 11.1 Utilize two turtles side-by-side on the main field to maximize the number of live swings.

The second type is game BP, which has already been discussed. The last type of batting practice is dual BP. We set up two portable batting cages side by side at home plate and place two frames in front of each portable cage. In the first cage, batters hit with less than two strikes. Their approach is to sit on a pitch that they are looking for up in the strike zone and to attack the inside part of the ball. If they do not like the pitch they are expected not to swing at it. The goal is to hit the ball hard with backspin consistently off the barrel. In the second cage batters hit with two strikes the entire time and do not know what pitch is coming. They make their four physical adjustments, and their approach is to be late on top. A right-hander should be hitting line drives and hard ground balls to the second-base side of the field, and a left-handed hitter should being doing the same thing to the shortstop side of the field. This drill is a good way to segment a hitter's approach to hitting by dividing his repetitions in half by the count. This type of BP simulates game conditions because hitters typically find themselves hitting with less than two strikes 50% of the time and with two strikes 50% of the time (table 11.1).

Table 11.1 Live Hitting: Simulated Games

1. Two-pitch/coach pitch scrimmage
2. Small game/bunt scrimmage
3. Integrated offensive components/batter scrimmage
4. Two-strike drill
5. Modified intrasquad games/scripted (LHP and RHP days):

Day 1: Groundball day: "Line drive down"	Day 2: RBI day/multiple runners: "Automatic"	Day 3: Bat control: "Move runners"	Day 4: Leadoff skills: "Get on base"	
			Game Rules: Points for bases advanced Reset situation after each batter Grade Intent, QAB's and Hard Contact String 5 Q-AB's together	**Adjustments:** Soft LHP velocity RHP Backwards guy No off-speed command Umpire strike zone

SIX-STATION BATTING PRACTICE

When setting up a hitting rotation, cover as many of the six elements of offense as possible. The focus should be strictly on offense; do not use a defense. Facilities play a big factor in what a team can accomplish. In this example we use the main playing field, a bunting corner, one full outdoor hitting tunnel, and two portable batting cages (figure 11.2).

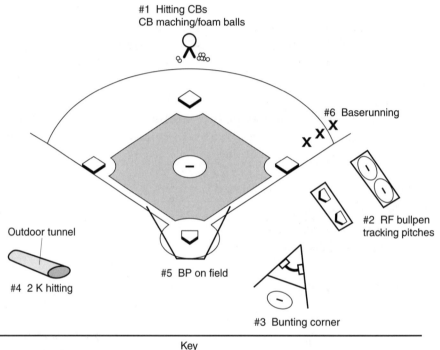

Key

1. CBs in CF, use ATEC foam balls
2. Tracking pitches in RF bullpen, work on load
3. Bunting corner, off pitching machine
4. Outdoor tunnel, off live arm, work on 2 K hitting
5. Batting practice on field
6. Base running on field

Figure 11.2 Six-station batting practice rotation.

Station 1

The first station is a curveball drill in center field. A portable batting cage is set up behind second base, home plate is in the dirt, and the batter is hitting toward center field. The pitching machine is 45 feet (13.7 m) away throwing curveballs using soft foam dimple balls that travel approximately 250 feet (75 m). The hitter's goal is to drive the curveball over the center-field wall. We want him to learn to wait for the elevated curveball with less than two strikes and drive it over the wall. The objective is for the hitter to gain confidence by learning to hit the "get me over" curveball with less than two strikes. The percentages indicate that hitters will get an off-speed pitch 80% of the time on the first pitch with a runner in scoring position, and they find themselves with runners in scoring position approximately 25% of the time. Championship teams can execute the two Bs—the bunting game and hitting the get-me-over breaking ball. Start from day 1 with these two skills because they will need to be there late in the season when it matters most.

Station 2

The second station is in the right-field bullpen. Hitters stand in the batter's box while the pitchers throw their bullpens. Vision and timing are the foundation of a productive hitter. Getting the opportunity to observe pitchers throwing live is a great way for hitters to practice these skills. When the hitter steps into the box we ask him to have open focus, to look at the pitcher but not focus on a particular point. The hitter is working on timing his load and getting in rhythm with the pitcher. If the pitch is a good one to swing at, he addresses the ball with his belly button, nods to the ball, and mentally completes the swing.

If the pitch is a ball, the hitter tracks the ball with his head and front shoulder all the way back to the catcher's mitt. We have a saying

Figure 11.3 The hitter "hawking" the ball all the way back into the catcher's mitt.

when it comes to vision: "See it longer, see it less." We want our hitters to "hawk" the ball (figure 11.3) on takes all the way into the catcher's mitt, or "see it longer." On contact, the hitter's chin should be down and over the contact area, and he leaves it down after contact, hence the phrase "See it less."

Station 3

This station is in the bunting corner. We use a pitching machine set in the upper 80s (about 140 km/h) with real baseballs that have Kevlar seams. These baseballs perform like leather baseballs, which helps the bunters get used to how the ball will exit the bat. The bunters work on the four primary bunts and run through a short base on their final bunt of each round. The goal is to create the proper pace and direction on each bunt. The bunting corner is marked off to give visual feedback on each bunt. Creating a competition is a good way to heighten the bunters' focus. Chart the bunts daily, rank the players from top to bottom, and post the rankings in the locker room.

Station 4

The outdoor tunnel is station 4 (figure 11.4), our two-strike station. The hitter starts with a 1-2 count and battles until the at-bat is completed. In Major League Baseball batters hit with two-strikes 49% of the time. Given those numbers we work on two-strike hitting every day. The BP pitcher mixes up the pitches, trying to strike out the batter. The batter makes his four two-strike physical adjustments and uses his two-strike approach, "late and on top."

Learning to put the ball in play with two strikes is critical for the high-scoring offense. The number one predictor for a big inning at the 2008 CWS was a two-strike base hit. We want hitters to feel confident when they are hitting with two strikes. Practicing this situation daily will help reduce the fear of the strikeout and minimize the panic that some hitters have of hitting with two strikes.

Figure 11.4 The outdoor tunnel can be used for a variety of drills, including two strike hitting off of a live arm or hitting curveballs off of a machine.

Station 5

Station 5 is on the main field with a BP pitcher. This station can be used in a variety of ways. An example would be the game-day BP routine, which incorporates hitting in various counts, changing speeds, executing with runners on base, and finishing each round with a bunt. In practice and on game day we chart batting practice and post the results in the locker room. This system helps hitters focus and lets them know that the coaches are paying attention to their ability to execute the skills that we think are important.

We vary the distance that the BP thrower is from the hitter to simulate the varying velocities of pitchers. For example, we know that a BP pitcher who throws approximately 51 miles an hour (82 km/h) and from a distance of 33.5 feet (10.2 m) from the hitter equates to a 92-mile-per-hour (148 km/h) fastball in terms of reaction time. By varying the distance of the BP pitcher from the hitter, we can work on rhythm and timing. (See the chart to calculate velocity from your BP pitchers.)

Velocity-simulated BP

Example: 92 mph (148 km/h) fastball with the BP pitcher throwing 51 mph (82 km/h)

Multiply 60.5 by 51 = 3,085.5 (18.4 m by 82 km/h = 1,508.9)

3,085.5/92 = 33.54 feet, the distance that the BP pitcher should be from the hitter to simulate 92 mph (1,508.9/148 = 10.2 m)

$$(A * B) / C = D$$

A = mound distance, 60 feet, 6 inches (18.4 m)

B = Radar velocity of BP pitcher, 51 mph (82 km/h)

C = Radar velocity of pitcher to face, 92 mph (148 km/h)

D = Feet (m) from hitter that BP pitcher should stand

Station 6

This station has base runners occupying every base and following a baserunning script. The base runners assume their primary leads at each base and start into their secondary leads when the pitcher's front foot lands. Lines are painted on the infield grass to help players execute their primary and secondary leads properly. When the ball is put in play the runners execute a four-step reaction. They are expected to get a read off the bat every third pitch. The runners at first and second react as if the next base is unoccupied. All runners react to pitches in the dirt. The runner at third reacts to the infield playing in with less than two outs and with the contact play on. Base runners rotate up one base when the hitter finishes a round. Incorporating a sliding pit into this station once a week is a good way to keep base runners sharp on this important skill.

TWO PITCH/COACH PITCH SCRIMMAGE

Two Pitch is much like batting practice in that the drill starts with a batting practice pitcher approximately 40 feet (12.2 m) from the hitter, half of the team on defense, and half of the team on offense. Five players hit and, depending on roster size, five guys run the bases. The drill starts with a situation (such as a runner at first base), and after four to six minutes the base runners and hitters switch and repeat the situation. This drill is primarily for the offense, but the defense, especially the outfielders, gets considerable work on their reads and making decisions on what base to throw to.

The greatest value of this drill is that base runners get live reads. They get multiple opportunities to make decisions on whether to tag or not and to vault back on head-high line drives. Because hitters are getting batting-practice fastballs, they are hitting numerous well-hit balls that allow base runners the opportunity to work on being decisive. After the play ends the situation is reset with a new base runner and a new hitter. After both groups finish, the defense and offense switch. A new situation can be created with both sides playing it live. After the play ends the situation is reset.

INTEGRATED OFFENSIVE COMPONENTS

Integrated Offensive Components (IOC) is a batting practice drill that simulates live game situations. Typical batting practice groups consisting of four or five hitters will be able to face all nine situations in approximately 10-12 minutes. After a group hits, they rotate and run the bases.

A hitter starts with a 1-1 count and attempts to execute in nine situations. Each situation has a mental strategy for success (buzz phrase) that the hitter repeats as he enters the cage. During this drill, the pitcher will vary his pitches based on the count. Also, the pitcher throws batting practice type stuff in order to enhance the hitters' confidence. If the hitter fouls off the first pitch, the count changes from 1-1 to 1-2 and hitter makes his two-strike adjustments. Alternatively, if the first pitch is a ball, the hitter moves into a positive count and is expected to drive the ball. Hitters rotate in and out after each live at-bat, just like a game. The base runners are matched up with a hitter, start at first base and follow the situational script.

IOC helps hitters learn the proper mental and physical strategy for each situation (first, first and second, first and third, and so on) in a slowed down environment. In addition, hitters learn to control the at-bat by understanding how the pitcher is trying to get them out in a slowed-down environment. This drill is also a useful baserunning drill. Each runner pairs up with a hitter and gets to run the bases in all nine situations. One thing to be aware of is that hitters hit around the ball with runners on base. Remind them that in almost all situations with runners on base they must attack the inside of the ball in order to be successful.

Variations of the drill can include:

1. Situation: nobody on base
   a. Goal: hit a 3-to-8 ball
   b. Reminder: "Your at-bat"

2. Situation: runner at first
   a. Goal: use four hole
   b. Reminder: "Big inning"

3. Situation: runner at first
   a. Goal: hit-and-run
   b. Reminder: "On top out of the middle"

4. Situation: runner at second base, no outs
   a. Goal: drive him over
   b. Reminder: "Right-side grass"

5. Situation: runner at second base, two-out RBI
   a. Goal: line drive down, up the middle
   b. Reminder: "L-frame"

6. Situation: runner at third base, infield back
   a. Goal: ground ball up the middle
   b. Reminder: "Play pepper"

7. Situation: runner at third base, infield in
   a. Goal: stay inside ball
   b. Reminder: "Automatic"

8. Situation: bases loaded, less than two outs
   a. Goal: opposite-field gap
   b. Reminder: "Knockout punch"

9. Situation: runners at first and third
   a. Goal: make the first baseman field the ball
   b. Reminder: "Safety squeeze"

MODIFIED INTRASQUAD GAMES

Every day that we play an intrasquad game we have a well-defined theme for the offense. We use one of four intrasquad formats, each of which features a specific objective for the hitter. After cycling through these four modified intrasquad games, hitters will have been exposed to almost every situation that they will ever face in a game.

The modified intrasquad format includes three offensive teams of five hitters each. All five hitters get their turns at-bat before the sides are rotated. After the play is completed the situation is reset so that all hitters get the same opportunity. Points are awarded to the offense for total bases advanced. Base runners are expected to steal within three pitches, and it is mandatory to go two bases on all base hits. We want to foster an environment of intelligent, aggressive baserunning and eliminate hesitation. We do not care if runners get thrown out; we just want them to learn what they can and cannot do in this controlled environment.

The first of the four intrasquad themes is "line drive down," so every hitter is expected to hit firm ground balls to move runners. Situations consist of a runner at second with no outs and a runner at third with the infield back. The final at-bat would be a two-strike at-bat with a 1-2 count, a runner at third, and the infield back. All hitters are expected to hit ground balls to move runners in all three situations. The feedback in the postpractice meeting is simple: If no routine fly balls were hit this day, chances are good that the offense had a productive day.

The theme for day 2 is "automatic," which means that hitters must stay inside the baseball and focus on the middle back side of the field. The situations are bases loaded and runners at first and third. The last at-bat would be a two-strike at-bat with the infield in. The approach for hitters throughout the intrasquad game is to look for a ball up in the zone and attack the inside part of the baseball, which facilitates driving the ball to the outfield. Hitters should lay off balls down in the zone, because those are pitcher's pitches that often lead to double plays.

The theme for day 3 is "move runners." Hitters face various situations in which their job is to put the ball in play and move the runner. The first situation is a runner at first base, and the batter executes a hit-and-run. The hitter's goal is to hit a ground ball out of the middle of the diamond, and he is required to swing at the pitch regardless of location. The second situation is a runner at second base with two outs, and the hitter's job is to hit a firm ground ball up the middle. If the ball goes through for a base hit, the batter–runner looks to take second on the throw home. In his final at-bat, the hitter starts with a 3-1 count and a runner is at first base. The hitter is expected to swing if the pitch is a strike and take the pitch if it is ball. The runner is stealing on the pitch.

The theme for day 4 is "get on base." Every hitter who comes up that day starts with nobody on base, so his job is to get on base. The challenge for the batter is to find a way to get on base any way he can, be it by a hit-by-pitch, bunt, walk, or base hit. The hitter knows that if he reaches base to start an inning with no outs the chance of his team scoring is 95%. Conversely, if he fails to reach base when leading off the inning, the offense has only a 30% chance of scoring.

The best thing about scripting intrasquads is that they afford every batter the same opportunity to execute. Additionally, coaches are able to gauge the accuracy of the batter's intent (approach) in each scenario. Another benefit is that the defense learns how to defend every conceivable scenario that might come up in a game. Because of the repetitive nature of the drill the coaching staff can evaluate every batter's at-bats in terms of whether he achieved a quality at-bat and whether he made hard ball contact (3-8 scale). These assessments are the only two that we make for hitters during intrasquad games. We rank players based on their quality at-bat percentage and highest hard ball contact at the conclusion of the fall season.

The modified intrasquad game gets its name from the division of the offensive team into three teams of five hitters. This modification is based on the fact that the average major-league inning consists of five batters. The hitters each get three at-bats, and all face the same situation. In the last at-bat the hitter starts with a 1-2 count and gets a maximum of two pitches. This at-bat is tacked on to the last round so that we only have to go around twice for each team to hit in all three situations. We do this not only to keep the flow of the game going but also to reinforce the concept of five batters attempting collectively to achieve five consecutive quality at-bats. Statistics show that one of the predictors of achieving a big inning is amassing five QABs in a row. We want these five-man teams working together as a unit, learning to string QABs together and understanding the value of passing the baton to the next hitter.

Again, teams earn points for each base reached, so every time that a batter–runner gains 90 feet (27.4 m) he earns a point for his team. At the end of intrasquad the team that has the most points wins. We want hitters and base runners to understand that every base matters. We want to promote the mentality that each man must do everything he can to advance himself around the bases, to do whatever he can to get an extra base. See table 11.2 for a template of the scrimmage scoring system.

Table 11.2   Scrimmage Scoring System

	Points	Team 1	Team 2
Pace of game			
Slow pace by pitcher and catcher	OT +2		
Off the field in 15 (OF) or 7 (IF) seconds	+2		
Between innings = 90 seconds	+2		
Around infield after strikeout > 5 seconds	OT +2		
Pitching			
Leadoff or two-out walk	OT +2		
No three-ball counts	+2		
Pick off runner	+2		
1-2-3-4-5 inning	+3		
Defense			
Less than 2 seconds by catcher between innings	+2		
Throw out lead runner with tag	+3		
Turn double play	+2		
No communication	OT +2		
Mental mistake	OT +2		
Error	OT +2		
Offense			
RBI	+2		
Bunt base hit	+2		
Dirt ball read	+1		
Two-strike base hit	+3		
Leadoff batter reaches	+3		
First to third	+2		
Eight-pitch at-bat	+2		
3-to-8	+2		
Draw a walk	+2		
Stolen base	+2		

	Points	Team 1	Team 2
Compete—toughness, effort, approach			
Flinch	OT +2		
Web gem	+2		
Nonhustle, failure to dive	OT +2		
Strikeout looking	OT +2		
Two-RBI pop-up	OT +2		
HBP	+		
Team battles			
Tally of bases advanced			
Winner of most bases advanced	+4		
Winner of freebie war (add)	+4		
Total			

OT equals other team.

From T. Guilliams, 2013, *High-scoring baseball* (Champaign, IL: Human Kinetics).

TWO-STRIKE

This particular two-strike drill has been modified from my college coach at Eastern Kentucky University, Jim Ward, who made our hitters go to the plate with a 1-2 count and face our ace pitcher. If we struck out we ran to the fence and back. This drill was the most challenging one I ever participated in, and we modified it to teach our players how to compete with two strikes.

Teams of five hitters compete against one another on the main field. The hitters bat twice and the pitcher throws a maximum of 20 pitches and then the sides then rotate. Each hitter starts with a 1-2 count and sees a maximum of two pitches. The hitter's job is to win two pitches. He does this by fouling off pitches, by putting the ball in play effectively, or by taking a pitch that results in a ball. We use a scoring system that awards points as follows: 1 point for a foul ball, 2 points for getting to a 3-2 count, 3 points for hitting ground-ball RBI, and 4 points for a base hit.

You can also start the drill with a runner at third and the infield back. In this scenario a hitter who can put the ball in play on the ground in the middle of the field will collect the RBI. This drill reinforces the concept that the RBI is more important than getting a base hit.

Additionally, we know that hitters get two strikes on them during half of their at-bats, so the final at-bat has the hitter start with a 1-2 count. The hitter who battles to a 3-2 count is now in control of the at-bat and has a 63% chance of getting a quality at-bat. The goal in this drill is to win pitches, stay alive, and ultimately put the ball in play effectively. Finally, it's important to note that hitters have a tendency to attack the ball too far out in front. Remind them to be "late and on top."

SMALL GAME

Small Game is a high-pressure, two-strike bunting drill in which half the team is on defense and half the team is on offense. The batters' goal is to get the ball in a kill zone and not only advance the runner but also get on base. The drill can be done with a live pitcher, a coach, or a machine. Always have a pitcher on the mound if a coach or machine is used. This drill is a great way for pitchers to practice fielding bunts. The drill starts with a runner at first base and a coach in the third-base coaching box giving the signs. The coach gives the bunter the sacrifice bunt sign, the batter bunts the ball to the first-base-side kill zone to advance the runner to second, and the defense records the out at first. With one out the next batter executes a drag bunt or push bunt to advance the runner. The bunter reaches base safely, and the next batter comes to the plate with runners at first and third. The coach gives the batter the sign for the safety squeeze. The batter does his job and makes the first baseman field the ball. The runner scores from third, and the out is recorded at first. The next batter comes up and performs a drag bunt. He is out on a close play for the third out of the inning. After the third out the next inning starts with a runner at first base.

After every player on the offense has an opportunity to bunt, the sides switch. A point is given for advancing a base, and two points are awarded for a run scored. Players have the opportunity to use bunts that are designed to get on base, to advance runners, and to score runners. We typically do this drill at second base and in shallow center field. The field is painted with kill zone lines and foul lines just as the bunting corner is. These lines help reinforce where we want players to bunt the ball. (See table 11.3 for a sample bunt scrimmage scoring sheet.)

Table 11.3 Bunt Scrimmage Scoring Sheet

Team #1 (offense)		Team #2 (bench)		Team #3 (defense)	
	C		C		C
	1B		1B		1B
	2B		2B		2B
	3B		3B		3B
	SS		SS		SS
	H		H		H
	H		H		H
	P		P		P
	P		P		P
	P		P		P
	P		P		P
	P		P		P
Total		Total		Total	
SCORING GRID					
+2 (other team)		+1, +2, +3			
Two foul balls and you are out		Base-hit bunt, safe		+2	
Popped-up bunt		Ball bunted in triangle		+2	
Error on the defense		Move runner		+1	
Mental error		Run scores		+2	
Nonhustle		Defense gets lead runner		+3	

From T. Guilliams, 2013, *High-scoring baseball* (Champaign, IL: Human Kinetics).

Table 11.4 Team Practice Schedule

#	Month	Date	Day	Prepractice	Base steal	Break down	Team defense	Situations	Lightning bolt	Teach game	Battle drill	Intrasquad	BP	Base run	Postpractice
1	Jan	10	Sun		Inside 1B	Square	Bunt 1st	Skip	1s & 2s				6 stations	3 spot	4 stations
2	Jan	11	Mon	BP		Square	Bunt 2nd	1Bs	1s & 2s				GM BP		4 stations
3	Jan	12	Tue	BP	Inside 2B	Square	Bunt 3rd	2Bs	1s & 2s				Dual		4 stations
4	Jan	13	Wed	GB		20 min	1st/3rd	Skip			SM GM		Stations	3 spot	
5	Jan	14	Thu	BP	at 1st 5 play	20 min	Drill series				SM GM		IOC live		
6	Jan	15	Fri	GB	at 2B		Trail picks			1 & 3/ load	SM GM		IOC live		
7	Jan	16	Sat	OFF											
8	Jan	17	Sun	1.5 run											Pictures
9	Jan	18	Mon	BP	1st/3rd	Pregame	Picks					#1 2K	GM BP		
10	Jan	19	Tue	BP		Pregame	Bunt					#2 Bunt	GM BP		
11	Jan	20	Wed	Square			Rundown/1-3				GB GM	#3 SR	GM BP		
12	Jan	21	Thu	Lift			Picks	Drill series	1s & 2s		SM GM		Dual BP		
13	Jan	22	Fri	GB		Pregame	Rundown/1-3					#4 Bunt	GM BP		
14	Jan	23	Sat	Blaz build	1st & 2nd	Pregame	Bunt					#1 2K	Dual		
15	Jan	24	Sun	Blaz blast	Off										
16	Jan	25	Mon	GB									4 station		Pregame
17	Jan	26	Tue	BP		Square	Bunt/1-3		1s & 2s		SM GM	#2	GM BP		
18	Jan	27	Wed	GB	3 spot		Bunt/1-3		Pregame			#3	4 station		
19	Jan	28	Thu	BP		Square			1s & 2s		SM GM	#4	GM BP		
20	Jan	29	Fri	GB	1-3 off		Bunt/1-3	Drill series		IOC live			4 station		
21	Jan	30	Sat	BP		Square	Picks		Pregame			LHPs	GM BP		Signs
22	Jan	31	Sun	OFF											
23	Feb	1	Mon	Game vs. Florida Tech, 1:00 p.m.											
24	Feb	2	Tue	Game vs. Florida Tech, 1:00 p.m.											
25	Feb	3	Wed	OFF											

Table 11.5 Offensive Checklist

Date: _____

Philosophy—seven runs							
Six elements of offense							
Bunting—master four							
Baserunning							
Base stealing							
Hitting, less than two strikes, two strikes							
Bat-control skills							
Slash							
Hit-and-run							
Hit-and-run drive							
Over and in							
Strike-zone discipline							
Goal: hit hard line drives, consistently, off the sweet spot of the bat with backspin							
Six phases of the swing							
Vision and timing							
Bat path and hand action							
Lower half and balance							
Approach: with less than two strikes, sit on what you're going to get up in the zone and attack the inside part of the ball							
Adjustments: "Ask LOUE" late, over, under, early							
Outcome: QAB, 3-8							
Two-strike adjustments: "Late and on top"							
Stress important play							
Hitting the curveball							
Positive count theory							
RBI situations—second, no outs; third, in; third, back; second, two outs; first and third; loaded							
Use middle of the field							
Cover high							
Hit-and-run philosophy—on the ground out of the middle							
Bases-loaded drill—keep ball off the ground							
THE FOUR PLAYS							
1. Get 'em on							
2. Get 'em over							
3. Get 'em in							
4. Keep rally going							

From T. Guilliams, 2013, *High-scoring baseball* (Champaign, IL: Human Kinetics).

Table 11.6 Sample Practice Plan

Date: _____

Stretch (2:30-2:50)	Baserunning checklist (2:50-3:05)	Throw (3:08-3:20)	Individual defense (3:20-3:40)	Team defense (3:43-4:13)	Competitive drills (4:16-4:36)	Offensive stations (4:41-5:56)	Scripted intrasquad (4:15-5:45)
	3		3	3	5	5	
Static stretch (6 min.) Ropes	Lead and return 1st 2nd 3rd	60—90—120 by position	Infield ___	Drill series one	Small game DP tee drill 2K hitting Live steals 27 outs Get on/over	Offensive BP Defensive BP Team BP S1 ___ S2 ___ S3 ___ S4 ___	Day 1 (LD down "GB day") 1. Drag 2. Over/in 3. 3rd back 4. 2K (Back
Active stretch 1. Form run • Low hurdles 2. Hurdles • Ladder • Dot 3. Agility • Box • Star • Pro • Shuttle 4. Arm care • Tubing • Weighted ball • Fungo	Secondary 22 feet 29 feet 21 feet	Infield Box drills	Outfield ___	Drill series two Rundowns Bunt defense 1st and 3rd Picks Street monkey		Game BP R1: Sac, H&R, O/I R2: GBs backside R3: LDs opposite R4: UTM LDs R5: 3-to-8	Day 2 (LD up "Automatic") 1. Push 2. 1st/ 3rd 3. Loaded 4. 2K (1st/3rd)
	Plays at 1st Secondary Steal Delay Fake break Hit and run	Outfield Single cuts Double cuts	Pitchers ___	Pregame UNF Game Cutoffs and relays Outfield throwing		Execution BP Free BP Off-set hitting IOCFDRS	Day 3 (RBI day) 1. Safety 2. 3rd in 3. 2 out RBI 4. 2K (3rd in)
	1st and 3rd Steal pullup Delay steal Get picked Early break	Catcher 1st 2nd 3rd	Catchers ___	Situations 1. Nobody/1B 2. At 1st/1B 3. At 1st – 2nd/1B 4. Nobody/2B 5. At 1st/2B 6. At 2nd/1B 7. At 3rd F-7 8. 1st/3rd Foul		Hitting rotation 1. Bunting (S, D, P, Q, SS) 2. Tunnel 1 3. Tunnel 2 4. Tees 5. Bat throws 6. Whirly-bird 7. Front toss 8. Side toss 9. CB machine 10. Special	Day 4 (Bat control) 1. Slash 2. Nobody on 3. Runner at 1st 4. 3-1 start runner
	Baserunning 1. One base • Home to 1st • Contact 2. Two bases • 1st to 3rd • 2nd to home	Pitcher Picks					
	Slides Bent Popup Head first Late/tap Dirt balls						

From T. Guilliams, 2013, *High-scoring baseball* (Champaign, IL: Human Kinetics).

CHAPTER 12

Game Day

I want them to remember that our most basic concept in preparing for games is the idea that you do not play an opponent; you play the game.

Andy Lopez, head baseball coach, University of Arizona

We share only a portion of the scouting report on the opponent with our players, and we do so after practice the day before the game. We mention a few of their strengths and weaknesses and share with the club their style of play. For example, do they like to run or are they a station-to-station team? We do not want any surprises on game day. We reinforce the importance of executing our system and remind our players that the biggest challenge is playing against the game, not our opponent. We always try to convey that we want our team to be on the offensive, to be in attack mode, to dictate the tempo of the game. We want the defense reacting to what we do, and we want the opponent concerned about us.

THE TEAM ATTITUDE

On game day in the locker room before the game we restate our baseball programs philosophy of TEAM—toughness, effort, approach, and master the fundamentals. Casey Stengel said, "I want players with brains and guts." We tell our players that when the game is over we want our report card to say that we earned an A in the things that we control. Those controllable elements are toughness, effort, and approach. The final component, mastering the fundamentals, is a work in progress that requires many hours of repetition. If we break down in any area, that final one is the only one in which we can accept less than an A. We understand that the game of baseball is a game of failure.

SCOUTING REPORTS

Scouting reports may help your team win a game. A detailed report may help your offense gain only an extra 90 feet (27.4 m) but that 90 feet may be enough to win the game. Scouting reports are based on charts of previous games and in-game observations. The reports are only as good as the data that are collected and the information that is extracted and ultimately put to use by the coaches and players. The information that we want to gather and share with the offense can be broken down into two parts: pitching and defense.

Pitching

The pitcher's control or lack thereof is the number one factor in the outcome of the game. The pitcher's control will affect offensive strategy. For example, an offense that is facing a pitcher who averages four or more walks per game may take more pitches than normal. The leadoff batter every inning might get the take sign if the first pitch to him is a ball to see whether the pitcher will fall even further behind and ultimately walk him. The offense may also decide to take pitches on 2-0 and 3-1 counts to run up the pitcher's pitch count.

Also, pitchers sometimes struggle with command of an off-speed pitch. If that happens the offense can eliminate that pitch from the pitcher's repertoire and sit on the fastball, especially in advantage counts. If the pitcher is a strike thrower, the offense may decide to use the hit-and-run more because they know that the pitcher will be around the plate, giving the batter something to handle.

Watching the pitcher warm up in the bullpen and during his initial warm-up on the mound before the start of the game can provide critical clues that can aid the hitters. For example, getting a read on the pitcher's arm slot can be useful. Is he straight over the top, high three-quarter, low three-quarter, or submarine? These arm slots each produce a different action on the baseball that the hitter needs to be aware of. In addition, pitchers will show a variety of secondary pitches in their warm-ups, such as an overhand curveball, slider, split finger, and straight change. Careful observation can enhance the hitters' ability to read and time his pitches.

Hitters must also closely observe how the pitcher is throwing to the other batters in the lineup. They should observe what pitch he likes to start hitters with, what pitch he throws with men in scoring position, what his command of his secondary pitches is, and what his put-away pitch is.

Control of the Running Game

The first thing that players and coaches want to know about the pitcher's ability to control the running game is his split time to the plate. The first time that a runner reaches first base we use a stopwatch to time the pitcher's pickoff move to first and his delivery time to the plate. Any pickoff move over 1.0 second means that we can extend our lead at first base, and any split time to the plate over 1.3 seconds is a green light for most of our base stealers. We also observe any patterns that the pitcher may have with his pickoff moves. The baserunning table (table 12.1) helps us record the following information.

- Does he pick to first base on his way up or on his way down?
- Does he only pick when he comes to his belt buckle?
- Does he look once or twice before he delivers to the plate?
- What is the pitcher's delivery time to the plate?
- What is the catcher's pop time to second base?

This information, coupled with knowledge of our players' speed, should give us an advantage in our base-stealing attempts. If a pitcher doesn't throw over much, he usually doesn't have a good move. Pitchers with good moves throw to first base often.

Table 12.1 Base-Stealing Tendencies Chart

Number		Pitcher	Team	Throws		Date	Charter
				L	R		
RUNNER AT FIRST BASE							
LHP				RHP			
Look at first, pick				Off rubber			
Look home, pick				Onto rubber			
Look at first, pitch				Going up			
Look home, pitch				At top			
Read				Coming down			
Step off				Set			
Delivery tempo, UCLA				Delivery tempo, UCLA			
PITCHER TIMES AT FIRST							
Stretch		Slide		Step		Pick	
RUNNER AT SECOND BASE							
No look				Inside move			
One look				Spin move			
Two looks				Timing			
Two plus two looks				No look			
PITCHER TIMES AT SECOND							
Stretch				Slide step			
Runner at first and third				Multiple runners			
Fake				Back pick			
PICKOFF ATTEMPTS							
First		Second				Third	
CATCHER							
Pop time to second base		Accuracy		Back picks (first base, second base, third base)		Blocking rating	

From T. Guilliams, 2013, *High-scoring baseball* (Champaign, IL: Human Kinetics).

Defense

The scouting report on the opponent's defense starts with the catcher's arm strength and accuracy. If the catcher throws extremely well the offense might use the hit-and-run instead of the steal. We also note whether the catcher likes to throw behind runners and how he blocks and retrieves.

As we go around the field we start with the outfielders. We want to know how strong their arms are and how quickly they unload the ball. Their skills will affect our ability to go from first to third on a single or stretch singles into doubles. We also share information about their decision-making ability and their ability to hit the cutoff man, which we can observe in pregame. These factors will help the trail runner know whether he can be aggressive in taking an extra base.

Next we focus on the arm strength of the middle infielders. If the middle infielders throw well then we might need to hold a runner on a ball hit into the gap because the middle infielders will be handling the ball and relaying it to home plate. But if the middle infielders demonstrate below-average arm strength, we might send the runner in that situation. We also keep a watchful eye on the movement of the middle infielders during the game. Specifically, with runners at first base we watch to see whether they are moving toward second base when the ball passes the hitter. If they are not, we may attempt a delay steal to exploit the middle infielders' inability to get to the bag on time. We also may run a fake break to see whether both middle infielders are breaking toward the second base. If they are, the hit-and-run is a good option because the middle of the diamond is wide open.

The corner infielders, particularly the third baseman, have a big effect on the decisions that the offense will make on game day. For example, how agile is the third baseman when fielding a slow roller? His ability will dictate how many times we will test him with our bunting game. Where does he position himself in relation to the hitter and the third-base bag? His positioning greatly affects his range, and we want to exploit that with our bat-control skills and short game. The first baseman's arm strength is also a factor. If he has a below-average arm we might run a first-and-third play to get the ball in his hands and exploit that weakness.

WARM-UP AND GAME BATTING PRACTICE

Before batting practice hitters should warm up prior to hitting on the field. A productive way to do this is to have the hitters take 30 to 40 swings in the cages. Besides getting the players warmed up so that they don't go to batting practice cold, the pregame hitting routine gets the players focused on the type of pitcher whom they are going to face that day.

For example, when the team will be facing a sinkerball pitcher, the routine would encompass hitting off low tees. The hitters need to focus on getting beneath the pitch and keeping it off the ground. When the opposing pitcher has an above-average fastball, the tees would be put in their highest position and the players would get in the mind-set of getting on top of the baseball. If they will be facing a soft lefty, the routine would have the players hit front toss from an extended distance to force them to let the ball travel its proper distance before they strike it. The objective is to increase the amount of time that they have to wait. If they will be facing a right-handed pitcher with a plus slider, an appropriate drill would be angled front toss so that the ball is cutting across the strike zone to a right-handed hitter. The batter keeps his front side down and in and drives the ball to the opposite gap. These four examples show how you can simulate different types of pitchers in your pregame hitting routine not only to warm up the players physically, but also to get them mentally focused on the type of pitcher whom they are going to face that day.

A pregame batting practice routine should get the hitter mentally prepared, get his timing honed, and get him kinesthetically aware of the bat head. Implementing the BP routine on the first day of fall will help the players memorize the routine so that they feel comfortable with it on game day. The routine should incorporate the six elements of offense (hitting with less than two strikes, hitting with two strikes, baserunning, base stealing, bunting, bat control, and strike-zone awareness). This routine reinforces to the players that repetition and proficiency in all elements of the offense are required for a high-scoring offense to fire on all cylinders. Each round of batting practice consists of five swings, and it ends when the batter executes a bunt and runs through a short base 30 feet (9.1 m) from home plate.

Group 1 will be on the field executing the scripted batting practice routine. Group 2 will be running the bases, group 3 will be in the bunting corner executing the five bunts, and the fourth group will be on defense. Have a strike zone for the on-field batting practice group so that the hitters can be aware of the strike zone. The scripted BP routine incorporates hitting with two strikes, hitting with less than two strikes, and bat-control skills. In addition, players get an opportunity to run the bases, and hitters see a variety of off-speed pitches with the aid of a strike zone or catcher. This routine, when practiced, can enhance the team's overall offensive production over the long run. In high school and college, batting practice should be viewed more as practice than a warm-up, because the typical college season of 50 games and the typical high school season of 25 games offer only a limited number of opportunities to get better. Listed in table 12.2 is an example of a scripted pregame batting practice routine.

Another idea to enhance pregame batting practice is to chart each swing to create a competition. The coach can post the results after each batting practice routine. See table 12.3 for a chart that the coach can use to teach players how to use the middle of the field, heighten their concentration, and create a fun competitive batting practice.

PREGAME MEETING

Before the game in the locker room, the coaching staff reviews the four offensive goals and the four defensive goals for the game. The focus is on what we control and how we execute the high-scoring offensive system. Our belief is that if we can achieve our game goals, victory is imminent. The game goals

Table 12.2 Scripted Pregame Batting Practice Routine

ROUND 1 (BAT CONTROL)
Shade: "Swing through the pitch"
Hit and run: "On the ground out of the middle"
Hit and run drive: "Drive the ball in the opposite gap"
Slash: "Pull bat back and pull the ball in the hole"
Drive 'em over: "Power ground ball to the right-side"
Drag
ROUND 2 (GRADUATE—EXECUTE 4-5 OFF OF THE GRASS)
Power ground balls off the opposite side grass
Push
ROUND 3 (CRIPPLE COUNTS 2-0, 3-1)
All FBs
Get your best swing off
"Sit on what you are going to get up in the zone and attack the inside of the ball"
Sac bunt 1B side
ROUND 4 (RBIS)
Runner at 2nd no outs:"Get 'em over"
Runner at 3rd infield back: "Play pepper with off middle infielder"
Runner at 3rd infield in: "Automatic" stay inside the ball
Bases loaded: "Knock-out punch" drive the ball to opposite gap
Runner at 2nd 2 outs: "L-frame" line drive down through the middle
Safety squeeze: Get an RBI with a bunt
ROUND 5 (TWO STRIKES)
Mix pitches
Hitters make two strike adjustments
Choke up
Move up
Get closer to the plate
Widen stance
Shorten stroke
3-2 count, start the runner: "Late and on Top"

provide direction for the team and serve as a benchmark to evaluate performance after the game. Emotions often run high in the postgame meeting, and comments can vary greatly. Game goals help create an atmosphere of a single-minded purpose: Did the team achieve one game goal on each side of the ball? This analysis eliminates the opponent and places the focus on competing against the game and evaluating the team's ability to execute the system. When we state the game goals they are supported by factual data that support those goals and reassure our players that if they execute, the results will take care of themselves.

Table 12.3 Batting Practice Game Score Sheet

Date: _____

Name	+5 HR cones	+4 Line L	+2 3-to-8 cones	+1 Hard, out	0 Weak, mid	-1 Average fastball	-2 Weak, out	-3 Foul, in	-5 Foul, out	-5 Cage	Total
1											
2											
3											
4											
5											
6											
7											
8											
9											
10											
11											
12											
13											
14											
15											
16											

SCORING GRID

0	Weak, middle	-1	Average fair fly ball, anywhere
+1	Hard hit, outside cones	-2	Weak, outside cones
+2	3 to 8 between cones	-3	Foul, inside the park
+4	Line-drive off the L-frame	-5	Foul, outside the park
+5	HR between cones	-5	Cage contact

From T. Guilliams, 2013, *High-scoring baseball* (Champaign, IL: Human Kinetics).

Four Offensive Game Goals

1. Seven runs
2. Big inning
3. Nine or more freebies
4. 50% quality at-bats

Four Defensive Game Goals

1. Four or fewer runs
2. Deny the big inning
3. Four or fewer freebies
4. 150 or fewer pitches

We remind the players that the offense is responsible for achieving one of the four offensive goals and the defense is responsible for executing one of the four goals on their side of the ball. If the offense and defense each attain one game goal, the result will be a victory 90% of the time. If the offense and defense each achieve two game goals, the result will be a victory 98% of the time.

The high-scoring offense focuses on achieving one game goal to obtain victory. The defense must achieve one defensive goal as well. The game of baseball is a zero-sum game, meaning that if the offense scores one run and the defense yields a run, the team is no further ahead. Yes, every team would like to have a high-scoring offense, but to achieve victory the defense must be proficient in minimizing the run production of its opponent. The goals for the offense and the goals for the defense are basically equal opposites. The factors inherent in run production are also evident in run prevention.

The great John Wooden did not use scouting reports. Instead, he believed that if his teams executed their philosophy correctly, they would emerge victorious regardless of who they played. We are trying to convey this mind-set: Execute the system. If we achieve one game goal on offense and one on defense, we will win 90% of our games.

FIVE SPRINTS

Even the simple act of running five sprints 15 minutes before the game can be a productive preparation time. When running the five sprints the players can work on the five plays that they should master from first base:

1. Secondary lead: two skips and react when the pitcher's front foot lands (no play)
2. Hit-and-run
3. Straight steal
4. Delay steal
5. Fake break

Use four lines of players leading off from the foul line. A coach serves as the pitcher, and the players walk off their leads depending on the play. If the coach attempts a pickoff throw, the players dive back into first, get up off the base, and get out to their leads again. The players execute the play, run 90 feet (27.4 m), jog back, and get back in line. This drill is a good mental exercise for the players as well as a good warm-up.

RULES OF ENGAGEMENT

Listed here are some guidelines for player conduct in the dugout, also known as the bunker, during the game:

1. The field is **sacred ground**, and all movement on the field will be **on the run**. All-out **sprint** to position, **jog** to the plate.
2. **No sitting** in the bunker, except the starting pitcher.
3. Everyone will **leave the bunker** to congratulate a teammate who scores or drives in a run.
4. **No** whining! **No** complaining! **No** excuses!
5. The on-deck batter will **verbally remind** the hitter of the proper **battle plan** (approach) required.
6. We will **never** show weakness. Always demonstrate the proper **combat stance**.
7. We are **always** on the **offensive**!
   Pitchers **attack** the strike zone.
   Fielders **attack** ground balls.
   Base runners **advance** themselves.
   Hitters take **controlled**, **violent** swings.
8. Players should always advance without stopping.
9. We play with **brains** and **guts**!
10. No matter what, **never** give up.

QUALITY AT-BAT CHART

The quality at-bat chart (figure 12.1) helps paint a detailed picture of what is transpiring during the game. Three boxes are provided for each at-bat for each hitter in the lineup. In the first box the count and the pitch that was put in play are recorded. The second box is used to record the result of the play and grade hard ball contact. In the last box a plus or minus is used to indicate whether the at-bat was a quality at-bat. At the completion of the inning the opposing pitcher's pitch count is recorded at the bottom half section of the chart. Also recorded are the total number of quality at-bats, the

	Name	#1			#2			#3			#4			#5			Total
1	Cormier	1-2 4 FB	1B 3	+	1-1 3 X	1B 4	+	1-0 2 FB	HR 7	+	0-0 0	IBB	+	0-0 1 X	3-U 2	−	4-5
2	Haney	0-0 1 FB	HR 7	+	2-1 4 FB	1B 2 •	+	1-0 2 SL	F-7 9	−	3-0 4	BB	+	2-1 4 FB	2B 7	+	4-5
3	Holmberg	0-0 1 FB	F-8 9	−	1-0 2 CB	6-4 2 •	−	0-0 1 FB	6-3 2	−	0-1 2 CB	2B 7	+	0-0 1 CB	F-9 9	−	1-5
4	Smith	0-2 3 SL	K 0 E	−	0-0 1 FB	5-4 2		2-0 3 SL	K 0-E	−	1-2 7 CB	HR 7	+	1-2 4 X	K 0 E	−	1-5
5	Greear	1-2 4 FB	6-3 2	−	0-1 2 CB	2B 7	+	0-2 3 FB	HBP	+	0-0 1 FB	1B 3	+	2-2 5 CB	K 0 E	−	3-5
6	Pyles	3-2 6 CB	K 0 E	−	1-2 4	F8 9	−	0-2 4 SL	K 0-E	−	3-0 4 X	BB	+	2-2 5 FB	2B 7	+	2-5
7	Roldan	1-1 3 SL	1B 5	+	0-2 3 FB	3-1 2 •	−	1-1 3 SL	F-7 9	−	1-1 3 SL	6-3 2 •	−	2-1 4 CB	L-9 7	+	2-5
8	Degnan/Swanson	0-1 1 SL	1-6-3 1	−	1-1 3 FB	2B 3	+	3-0 4 FB	BB	+	3-2 6 CB	BB	+	3-2 8 FB	K 0 L	+	3-4/1-1
9	McLeod	1-1 3 FB	F-9 9	−	0-1 2 FB	SAC DRAG	+	0-0 1 FB	SAC BUNT	+	0-0 1 FB	F-9 9	−				2-4

QABs	Base hit	3-to-8	8 pitches	BB	RBI	Well-placed bunt	Advanced runner	HBP

Pitches		Innings	At-bats	Quality	String	Runs	Comments
13		1	5	2	2	2	2-run HR
10	23	2	3	1	1	0	GIDP in a positive count
13	36	3	5	2	2	0	Pull, pull, pull
9	45	4	3	1	1	0	Bad baserunning
10	55	5	5	3	3	2	2-run HR
13	68	6	4	1	1	0	Early with 2 strikes
18/15	86	7	11	9	8	5	Knockout punch by Holmberg
10	25	8	4	1	1	1	E9 scored a run
	22	9	4	3	3	1	Wild pitch to 3rd
		10					

Total QAB	QAB %	Under	Total 3-to-8	3-to-8 %	< 2K 3-to-8 %	E/U w/ 2K	Big three			Big innings
23-44	52%	4	13-36	36%	(10-23) 43%	(7-15) 47%	5	7	0	1

	#	Name	R/L	#	Name	R/L	#	Name	R/L	#	Name	R/L
Time 1B/2B												
K Pitch												
Pattern												
FB/CB/X												
Plan												

Figure 12.1   Quality at-bat chart.

Grading period/Game: _____/_____ Opponent: _____ Date: _____

	Name	#1				#2				#3				#4				#5				Total
1																						
2																						
3																						
4																						
5																						
6																						
7																						
8																						
9																						

QABs	Base hit	3-to-8	8 pitches	BB	RBI	Well-placed bunt	Advanced runner	HBP

Pitches		Innings	At-bats	Quality	String	Runs	Comments
		1					
		2					
		3					
		4					
		5					
		6					
		7					
		8					
		9					
		10					

Total QAB	QAB %	Under	Total 3-to-8 %	3-to-8 %	< 2K 3-to-8 %	E/U w/2K	Big Three		Big Innings

	#	Name	R/L	#	Name	R/L	#	Name	R/L	#	Name	R/L
Time 1B/2B												
K Pitch												
Pattern												
FB/CB/X												
Plan												

From T. Guilliams, 2013, *High-scoring baseball* (Champaign, IL: Human Kinetics).

Figure 12.2 Quality at-bat chart template.

number of quality at-bats that were strung together, and the number of runs scored that inning.

The quality at-bat chart serves as the primary tool to evaluate the offense on their ability to execute the system. From this chart players and coaches will be able to extract the following information:

1. Quality at-bat percentage
2. Two-strike quality at-bat percentage
3. Hard ball contact (3-to-8)
4. How many times the offense strung together five quality at-bats
5. Total pitch count of the opposing pitcher
6. Percentage of the time that hitters had two strikes
7. Whether the offense had a big inning
8. The number of free bases accumulated by the offense
9. The part of the lineup (e.g., top three hitters, middle three hitters, or last three hitters) that was the most productive in terms of quality at-bats

IN-GAME ADJUSTMENTS

The first element that the offense will have to adjust to on game day is the umpire's strike zone. The strike zone is not what is in the rule book but what the umpire says it is. The umpire's strike zone has a great influence on game strategy. If the umpire has a small zone, batters can tighten their hitting zone and wait for a good pitch to hit. On the other hand, if the umpire has a large strike zone, hitters will have to expand their hitting zone and have a good two-strike approach. When the umpire's strike zone is small, game strategy may call for use of the take sign. The opposite would hold true if the strike zone is large. In that case hitters have to be more aggressive and move in the batter's box to adjust to the "real" strike zone. Adjusting to the umpire's strike zone is important for the high-scoring offense.

The second adjustment that the offense must make is to understand how the pitcher is trying to get each hitter out. If the pitcher is consistently throwing pitches on the outer half of the strike zone, the hitter will have to move closer to the plate to hit the ball to the opposite-field gap. The hitter should have the mentality that the pitcher controls only where the hitter hits the ball, not how hard he hits it. If the pitcher is throwing the batter a steady diet of curveballs, the hitter should move up in the box and sit on the curveball. With less than two strikes the hitter is looking for the curveball up in the zone. With two strikes, depending on the umpire's strike zone, the hitter may have to get on top of the plate and take away the outside corner.

Baseball is a game of adjustments. High-scoring offenses can make immediate adjustments to the umpire's strike zone and to the way in which the pitcher is trying to get each hitter out. The offense does not wait until the seventh inning to start making adjustments. At the higher levels of baseball, the players make in-game adjustments quickly. Average hitters make adjustments game to game, good hitters make adjustments at-bat to at-bat, and great hitters make adjustments pitch to pitch. Just remember to follow the acronym LOUE from chapter 5 when players are adjusting their plan with each pitch.

CHAPTER 13

Team Evaluation

I think accurate and detailed record keeping is most important in leadership. I was always looking for clues that would help us improve individually and as a team. To help me accomplish this, I also kept extensive and detailed accounts of practice and games.

John Wooden, former head basketball coach at UCLA and winner of 10 national championships

Keeping accurate and detailed reports on the components that make up a high-scoring offense provides coaches and players with information that can help them better execute the system and stay on course over the entire season. It has been said that if you want to get better, measure it. This chapter delves into evaluating both the individual hitter and the collective effort of the offense during the fall season, spring games, and postgame. The evaluation process ends by using a team grade card in conjunction with grading periods.

FALL SEASON

During the fall season the players are evaluated on their individual offensive productivity through two primary statistics: their quality at-bat percentage and their (3-to-8) hard ball contact percentage. The players' ability to obtain a QAB is the foundational building block of a high-scoring offense. The hard ball contact grade is a better predictor of future success than batting average because of the limited number of at-bats (about 40) that hitters get in fall. Batting average is not only overvalued in terms of determining a hitter's productivity but also can paint an unrealistic picture of performance when the number of at-bats is limited. In the book *Moneyball*, Voros McCracken concluded that

> pitchers had no ability to prevent hits, once the ball was put in play. They could prevent home runs, prevent walks, and prevent balls from ever being put into play by striking out batters. And that, in essence, is all they could do. (Lewis, 2003)

The point for hitters is that hard ball contact is a better evaluator than batting average of their future offensive productivity. This also falls in line with our overall hitting philosophy that the goal is not to get a hit but to hit the ball hard, thereby achieving a quality at-bat, which is the only thing a hitter has control over.

The final area on which we evaluate individual hitters is their walk-to-strikeout ratio, and we add HBPs to their walk total. The results are posted every week and tallied at the end of the fall season. Our hope is that we see constant improvement throughout the fall and that, ultimately, a player walks more often than he strikes out. An exceptional player may walk twice as often as he strikes out. This statistic emphasizes to players that the walk is the second greatest play in baseball and that the strikeout is the second worst play in baseball. During intra-squad games players are grouped into three teams of five players. Each inning consists of five batters, the length of an average major-league inning. Those five players have the goal of stringing together five quality at-bats, setting the table for a big inning. Overall, the three teams of five players get two live at-bats, one with an 0-0 count and one with a 1-1 count, for a total of 30 at-bats. The goal is to accumulate 15 quality at-bats (50%) for the day. The intra-squad game ends with the players getting one at-bat with a 1-2 count and a runner at third base. This bonus round is not used in their overall QAB percentage. Aggressive and intelligent baserunning is encouraged by awarding points for total bases advanced. The two losing teams receive pick-ups based on the number of points by which they lose. We want the players to advance on every ball in the dirt, to go from first to third on every base hit, and to score from second on every potential RBI. This system not only helps players learn what they can and cannot do but also applies immense pressure on the defense to execute.

Almost every intra-squad game ends with a two-strike round in which the hitter starts with a 1-2 count, a runner on third base, and the infield back. The hitter's goal is to put the ball in play on the ground to score the runner from third. This drill focuses on the importance of winning pitches and getting to a three-ball count. After the hitter gets to a three-ball count we give the offense one point and bring the next hitter to the plate. A hitter's chance of getting a QAB rises from a 37% chance with two strikes to a 74% chance with a three-ball count.

The players are trying to reach several goals by the conclusion of the fall season:

1. 60% individual QAB
2. 50% 3-to-8 hard ball contact percentage
3. 2:1 walk-to-strikeout ratio

All this information is used in player evaluation after the fall season to help each player understand what he did well and what he needs to improve on before the start of the spring season.

DURING GAMES

The quality at-bat chart (refer to figure 12.1) and the pitcher tendency chart (table 13.1) are the two primary tools that serve to enhance the hitter's ability to be a productive offensive player during games. These two charts are kept during games to look for patterns in the offense and in the opponent's pitching staff that can be used to gain a competitive advantage. In-game adjustments are critical for the offense; a team must be spontaneous and flexible to achieve one of its four game goals.

To help reinforce the concepts of a high-scoring offense, a separate chart is kept to record the five ways that a player can earn a helmet decal for his performance on game day:

1. Leadoff batter reaches safely.
2. Earn a freebie and score.

Table 13.1 Pitcher Tendency Chart

Team:		Date:	Game number:	Start/relief number:	Catcher:
Pitcher:		Number:	Class:	Innings:	Number:

R L

Hitter	Ahead in count						Behind in count			Even in count		Full count	Base-runners	AB result
Count	0-0	1-0	2-0	2-1	3-0	3-1	0-1	0-2	1-2	1-1	2-2	3-2		
1														
2														
3														
4														
5														
6														
7														
8														
9														
PH														
PH														
PH														
PH														

Totals	Ahead in count						Behind in count			Even in count		Full count	1st pitch RBI	1st pitch empty
Count	0-0	1-0	2-0	2-1	3-0	3-1	0-1	0-2	1-2	1-1	2-2	3-2		
FB														
CB														
CH														
Slider														
Other														

DESCRIBE (MOVEMENT, VELOCITY, LOCATION AND COMMAND)

FB	Slider
CB	Other
CH	K pitch

From T. Guilliams, 2013, *High-scoring baseball* (Champaign, IL: Human Kinetics).

3. Two-strike quality at-bat.

4. Collect an RBI.

5. Perfect day! All plate appearances result in a quality at-bat.

Recognizing outstanding player performance by awarding helmet decals has been primarily a football device. Borrowing that theme, we recognize a hitter's ability to perform one of these five offensive contributions to a high-scoring offense by rewarding him with a batting helmet sticker. These five categories play a significant role in the team's ability to score seven runs per game. As previously mentioned, if the leadoff batter reaches base safely the offense has a 95% chance of scoring. We also know that a two-strike base hit is the number one predictor of a big inning, so we certainly want to reward players when they make that contribution.

Game Execution Chart

The game execution chart is a detailed account of the game (figure 13.1). This chart tracks every individual component that the coaching staff believes affects the team's ability to produce runs and prevent runs. Hitters are evaluated in 18 categories and base runners are evaluated in 11 categories. This level of detail is critical in dissecting the execution of skills that make up a high-scoring offense. Each category has nine boxes, and each box has two spaces. The top space is for the player's number, and the bottom space is for a plus or minus. The chart promotes accountability because it identifies those who execute the skills and those who fail to execute. At the end of the chart a space is provided to tally overall execution in each of the four areas of the game. The total in each category reflects either a positive or a negative outcome in the respective categories. Spaces are also provided for game totals in each of the four offensive and defensive game goals.

The game execution chart works in conjunction with the quality at-bat chart to provide a high level of detail about offensive execution, both individually and as a team. The game execution chart helps the coaches paint a picture of what actually occurred during the game. By using both of these charts the players and coaches have a good understanding of what factors contributed to run production and run prevention. The information that is pulled from the chart is used to make adjustments before the next game and the next team practice. (See www.humankinetics.com/hkmedialibrary/hk_media_library/high-scoring-baseball-tables for a template of the game execution chart.)

Opponent:_____   Date/Game:_____

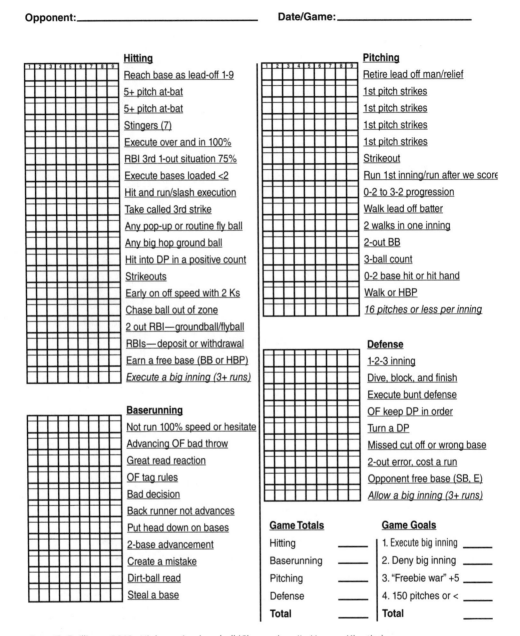

Hitting

Reach base as lead-off 1-9
5+ pitch at-bat
5+ pitch at-bat
Stingers (7)
Execute over and in 100%
RBI 3rd 1-out situation 75%
Execute bases loaded <2
Hit and run/slash execution
Take called 3rd strike
Any pop-up or routine fly ball
Any big hop ground ball
Hit into DP in a positive count
Strikeouts
Early on off speed with 2 Ks
Chase ball out of zone
2 out RBI—groundball/flyball
RBIs—deposit or withdrawal
Earn a free base (BB or HBP)
Execute a big inning (3+ runs)

Baserunning

Not run 100% speed or hesitate
Advancing OF bad throw
Great read reaction
OF tag rules
Bad decision
Back runner not advances
Put head down on bases
2-base advancement
Create a mistake
Dirt-ball read
Steal a base

Pitching

Retire lead off man/relief
1st pitch strikes
1st pitch strikes
1st pitch strikes
1st pitch strikes
1st pitch strikes
Strikeout
Run 1st inning/run after we score
0-2 to 3-2 progression
Walk lead off batter
2 walks in one inning
2-out BB
3-ball count
0-2 base hit or hit hand
Walk or HBP
16 pitches or less per inning

Defense

1-2-3 inning
Dive, block, and finish
Execute bunt defense
OF keep DP in order
Turn a DP
Missed cut off or wrong base
2-out error, cost a run
Opponent free base (SB, E)
Allow a big inning (3+ runs)

Game Totals

Hitting   _____
Baserunning   _____
Pitching   _____
Defense   _____
Total   _____

Game Goals

1. Execute big inning   _____
2. Deny big inning   _____
3. "Freebie war" +5   _____
4. 150 pitches or <   _____
Total   _____

Figure 13.1 Game execution chart.

Game Goals

During the postgame meeting in the locker room, coaches review the team's ability to achieve the four offensive game goals:

1. Achieve one big inning (three or more runs)
2. Earn nine or more freebies
3. Score seven runs
4. Collect 50% quality at-bats

The team understands that by achieving one goal on offense and one goal on defense they will win 90% of their games. Our primary focus is to execute the system, so we evaluate players on their ability to do so. Although it rarely happens, if the team loses after executing one goal on offense and one goal on defense, we tip our hats to the opponent. But if we lose and do not achieve one of the four offensive goals, we discuss why we failed and what adjustments we need to make before the next game. For example, if we have 40 at-bats during the game and amass only 18 QABs, simple math tells us that we are 2 quality at-bats away from reaching our goal of 50%. Breaking it down in this manner illustrates how important each at-bat is during the game. Focusing on game goals provides direction for the discussion and keeps the team focused on competing against the game rather than the opponent.

GRADE CARDS

A giant grade card is posted in the locker room. On that card are listed the four offensive goals and four defensive goals, which are marked by a plus or minus to indicate whether the team achieved that goal for that particular game. Following the game goals, the offense is broken down into the six ways to create offensive pressure, followed by the "big three" (the three worst outs in baseball), followed by a line for defensive errors. Each category has a corresponding goal that the team is trying to reach. For the defense the goal is one error or less. This challenging goal is achievable and is indicative of championship teams. Finally, we list six pitching categories and corresponding goals for each that we believe are the most important in terms of run prevention. The grade card is updated after each game so that players can observe how the team performed. Figure 13.2 provides an example of what a team grade card might look like.

Year 2008   Record 5-2   Grading Period CWS

W/L	#	Team	Offensive goals				Defensive goals				Offensive pressure						Big three			Pitching					
			Big inning	Free-bies +8	7 runs	QAB 60%	Deny Big inning	Free-bies -4	4 runs or <	140-160 P	Bunt ≤3	Chase 21%	BB 3	3-8 50%	QAB 60%	BB HBP 6	Over 4	Under 2	KL 0	1st pitch Ks 58%	3-ball count 6	Lead-off out 87%	P per inning 16	BB HBP 2	WHIP 1.3
W	1	Rice	+	+	+	–	–	–	–	+	0-0	23%	1-1	38%	52%	8	10	3	3	46%	7	33%	14	5	1.67
W	2	North Carolina	–	+	–	–	–	+	+	+	3-3	20%	3-3	33%	51%	5	13	2	2	48%	6	56%	16	2	1.4
L	3	North Carolina	–	–	–	–	+	–	+	–	0-0	30%	0-0	25%	39%	4	6	5	1	59%	11	56%	19	6	1.5
W	4	North Carolina	–	+	–	–	+	+	+	+	1-4	31%	1-1	28%	55%	11	9	2	1	66%	8	67%	14	3	1.4
L	5	Georgia	+	–	–	+	–	+	–	+	0-1	34%	0-0	30%	46%	5	9	8	0	50%	5	63%	14	2	1.5
W	6	Georgia	+	+	+	–	–	–	–	–	0-0	21%	1-2	43%	63%	9	10	6	2	53%	8	44%	20	7	2.4
W	7	Georgia	+	–	–	–	+	–	+	+	1-2	29%	0-1	42%	50%	3	5	6	1	63%	5	67%	16	3	1.0
		Totals	4	4	2	1	3	3	4	5	1	35%	1	27%	52%	6	9	5	1	55%	7	53%	16	4	1.32

Figure 13.2   Team grade card example.

OFFENSIVE PRESSURE

A high-scoring offense can create pressure in six ways:

1. Well-placed bunts (3)
2. Stolen bases (3)
3. Chase % <21%
4. Quality at-bat percentage with men in scoring position (60%)
5. Walks and HBPs (6)
6. Hard ball contact (3-to-8) percentage with less than two strikes (50%)

The coaching staff keeps track of the six ways that an offense can create pressure to monitor the level of proficiency that the offense demonstrates during games. A pattern often develops that alerts the coaching staff that an adjustment needs to be made and that more time needs to be spent on certain areas in practice. Each area has a specific objective, represented in parentheses above, that the offense is trying to achieve each game. Not only do those offensive pressure objectives provide direction, but they also serve as a way to evaluate the team.

BIG THREE

We also track what we call the big three:

1. Over (big-hop ground balls): goal of four or less
2. Under (routine fly balls): goal of two or less
3. Strikeout looking: goal of none for the game

We borrowed the idea of the big three from the legendary Ron Polk, former head coach at Mississippi State University. These three types of outs create no pressure on the defense and must be minimized if the offense is to be productive. A big-hop ground ball makes contact in the dirt circle in front of home plate, which slows it down and increases the range of an infielder. The ball usually takes several large hops, allowing the infielder to field it above his knees. The University of Florida assistant baseball coach Brad Weitzel said, "If an infielder fields a ground ball above his knees, it might as well be a fly ball." Routine fly balls create no pressure and are generally the easiest outs for the defense to record. Although the ultimate goal is to have zero big-hop grounders during the game, we will tolerate four or fewer in a nine-inning ballgame. The last of the big three is a strikeout looking, for which our goal is zero because we know that striking out looking in no way helps the team at least move a runner. Strikeouts looking must be avoided at all costs.

Each of these unproductive outs provides information to the coaching staff and feedback to the hitters in terms of adjustments that need to be made. Ernie Rosseau, former head baseball coach at Brevard Community College in Melbourne, Florida, stated, "We're a nation of over/under hitters." Rosseau's point, essentially, is that hitters tend to overspin balls to the pull side and to be under to the back side of the field. This swing flaw is called a barrel flop. The barrel enters the strike zone below the flight of the pitch and is then flopped up to the ball, which creates these unproductive outs. By tracking these outs, the coaching staff has data to support their findings that the hitters have a propensity for the number one swing flaw—the barrel flop. This information can be used as a base line and can help reduce the number of over and under outs that occur throughout the season.

Baseball is all about failure, and tracking how the offense is making outs allows the coaching staff to understand what the team needs to do to create pressure on the opposition. For example, hitting the ball hard and flat takes away the reaction time of the defense and creates the most pressure. Also, eliminating strikeouts looking and putting the ball in play more often can cause the defense to make more mistakes. The high-scoring offense puts the ball in play more consistently and with more authority than a less dynamic offense does. Each team only has 27 outs with which to work. The goal is to make the defense work extremely hard to record all 27 outs. We want to avoid the big three as much as possible.

GRADING PERIODS

To improve the team's ability to perform consistently over a long season, we break the baseball season into five grading periods (table 13.2). The NCAA II spring season consists of 50 games, which we break into five grading periods of 10 games each. The goal for wins and losses for each 10-game grading block is 8 wins and 2 losses. If the team meets the goal in each grading period, they would end the regular season with 40 wins and 10 losses. Breaking the season into five equal grading periods helps the team stay focused on the present. Players are evaluated after every 10-game period individually and collectively. The coaching staff discusses things that the players did well and the things that they need to improve on for the next 10 games. A primary benefit of the 10-game grading periods is that players can leave a bad 10-game block behind. Coaches can communicate to a player that a poor grading period is over and then give him specific goals for the next 10-game stretch. The obvious goal is improvement. For example, the shortstop may make six errors in the first 10 games of the season but make just one error over the next 10. He obviously has made progress, although his overall statistics would not reflect a dramatic improvement. The players and the coaches know that he is much better today than he was 10 games ago.

Table 13.2 Grading Periods (Five)

		2002	2003	2004	2005	2006	2007	2008	2009
1	1-10	8-2	8-2	10-0	9-1	8-2	8-2	7-2-1	8-2
2	11-20	9-1	9-1	10-0	10-0	6-4	8-2	6-4	6-4
3	21-30	8-2	8-2	9-1	9-1	8-2	9-1	8-2	8-2
4	31-40	8-2	10-0	6-4	7-3	10-0	8-2	6-4	7-3
5	41-50	7-3	6-4	8-2	6-4	8-2	8-2	6-4	8-2
Postseason		9-2	7-5	9-3	10-3	6-3			6-4
Totals		49-12	48-14	52-10	51-12	46-13	41-9	33-16-1	43-17

Every 10 games, goal is 8-2

Our ultimate goal is to continue to improve and play our best baseball at the end of the year. A useful aspect to these 10-game mini-seasons is that they mirror the postseason. Typically, a team plays approximately 10 to 12 games in the postseason. The concept of grading periods can be easily adapted to high school. Coaches can break the 30-game season into five periods of 6 games each. According to John Wooden, accurate and detailed record keeping is critical in helping players improve.

KNOW YOURSELF

How well do the players know themselves and how well do the coaches know the players? These are critical questions that must be answered in the evaluation process. As Suz Tzu said in the *Art of War*, "If you know the enemy and know yourself, you need not fear the result of 100 battles."

Players and coaches get to know themselves better through proper evaluation. As the saying goes, if you want to get better, measure it. The evaluation process for a high-scoring offense can be broken down into three areas. First, how well has the team accomplished the four game goals? This is done through the use of the game execution chart and the quality at-bat chart. Data is extracted from these charts to fill in the second element, the grade card. The grade card paints the picture of how well a team executes the system, not only for individual games but also for the previous 5 to 10 games, depending on the length of that team's season. The grade card helps to identify areas that the team and players need to improve upon and reinforces areas that are strengths. Finally, consolidating this information into five regular-season grading periods helps players and coaches stay focused on the season in smaller, more manageable blocks of time.

An ongoing, consistent evaluation process is valuable for three critical reasons. First, it affords the coaching staff an opportunity to make adjustments in the practice plan based on the factual data that is in the grade card.

Secondly, this information helps individual players make mechanical and mental adjustments to better execute the system. And, finally, it provides an opportunity for positive reinforcement through rewarding players with helmet decals at the end of each grading period.

It's all about getting better and the game is the best teacher. Collecting detailed and accurate information helps keep individuals and coaches on track throughout the course of a long season. Evaluation and adjustments are what make ordinary offenses high-scoring offenses. The ultimate goal is to be playing your best baseball at the end of the year. Through constant evaluation, making timely adjustments, and focusing on executing the four game goals, the high-scoring offense will be firing on all cylinders at the right time…tournament time!

References

Blanchard, K. and D. Shula. (2001). *The Little Book of Coaching*. HarperBusiness.

Felber, B. (2005). *The Book on the Book*. New York: St. Martin's Press.

Horne, R. (1999, Spring). *USC's Boys of Summer—Team of Destiny*. Retrieved April 18, 2012, from University of Southern California Trojan Family Magazine: http://www.usc.edu/dept/pubrel/ trojan_family/spring99/baseball/baseball2.html

Keri, Jonah, ed. (2006). *Baseball Between the Numbers*. Prospectus Entertainment Ventures LLC, Basic Books.

Lewis, M. (2003). *Moneyball*. New York: W. W. Norton & Company, Inc.

NCAA. (2011). *NCAA Division I Baseball Statistics Trends (1970-2011)*.

Pavlovich, Lou, Jr. "Power of the Lowly Walk." *Collegiate Baseball* 17 April 2009: 1, 6-7.

Robinson, Jackie, in a 1966 edition of *Sport Magazine*.

Robson, Tom. (2003). *The Hitting Edge*. Champaign, IL: Human Kinetics.

Small ball. (2002, October 11). *Collegiate Baseball*, p. 6.

Springer, Steve. *Quality At-Bats: The Mental Side of Hitting*. [audio CD].

Tango, T., Lichtman, M., & and Dolphin, A. (2007). *The Book*. Dulles, VA: Potomac Books.

Will, George. (1990). *Men at Work*. New York: Harper Perennial.

Williams, P. (1997). *The Magic of Teamwork*. Nashville, TN: Thomas Nelson.

www.everything2.com. (2008, June 28). Retrieved from http://everything2.com/title/ Pythagorean+Theorem+of+Baseball

About the Author

Coach **Todd Guilliams** joined the staff of the Valdosta State University baseball team in 2008 and helped orchestrate one of the top 10 turnarounds in the country in Division II, taking the Blazers to a 36-18-1 record in 2008 and following up with a 43-21 mark in 2009 and a 43-17 record in 2010. As the team's hitting and catching coach, Guilliams has put together one of the most prolific offenses in Valdosta State history, breaking the school record for batting average in 2010 with a .351 mark. In 2009 the squad led the nation and set a Valdosta State record with 113 home runs, ranking fourth in NCAA Division II history while finishing eighth nationally for the season with 578 runs scored.

Before joining Valdosta State, Guilliams helped his brother Greg build a dynasty at Embry-Riddle, where the program won 622 games against just 228 losses, making six NAIA World Series appearances in the process. He served as the team's hitting, catching, and outfield instructor, which produced 44 NAIA All-America selections. In the 15 years that Guilliams coached at Embry-Riddle, it was the winningest baseball program at any collegiate level (junior college, NAIA, Division I, or Division II) in the state of Florida. His run at Embry-Riddle was briefly interrupted as he spent the 2000 season as an assistant with Dallas Baptist. During his year with the Patriots, the team registered a 43-23 record and advanced to the NAIA World Series, where it finished as national runner-up.

Guilliams began his coaching career as a graduate assistant at Eastern Kentucky University in 1989 and 1990. The Colonels won an Ohio Valley Conference championship in 1989 and posted a 42-15 record in 1990. He spent three seasons as an assistant coach with the Staunton Braves in the Valley League from 1990 to 1992. Throughout his 28 years in college baseball he has authored articles published in *College Baseball Digest* and twice has been a featured speaker at the American Baseball Coaches Association national convention. He's also made presentations at high school baseball coaches association clinics in Georgia, Alabama, and Ohio. His instructional videos are available at www.MyCoachOnline.com.